From Priest to Police:

REFLECTIONS OF A JOURNEYED SOUL

Barbara —

Thank you so much for all of your kindness —

with warmest regards —

by *Chick Pritchard*

Chick Pritchard

Printed in the United States of America
First Printing, 2022

DEDICATION

This book is dedicated to my wife, Donna. I have wanted to write these words for many years, but without her encouragement, patience and enthusiasm, this memoir would not have been completed. I am thankful for her advice and suggestions. I am more grateful for her love and support.

Disclaimer

Dear Reader:

This book is a memoir. It depicts actual events in the author's life. The events are portrayed to the best of my memory. They are as true as my recollection permits. They represent my best memory of past experiences. Conversations from my past are not written to represent word-for-word transcripts of discourse. They have been retold in a way that remains true to the context of the conversation. While all persons are actual individuals, the names and identifying details of some have been changed to protect their privacy. Respectfully,

Chick Pritchard

CONTENTS

Acknowledgments

There are numerous members of my family and friends who took time out of their busy schedules to read some of these words, but more especially, to encourage me as I wrote. They know who they are. I am forever grateful to each one of you.

I am also very indebted to Ms. Aline Demeusy, the talented artist who created my cover design. She is uniquely gifted. Her work beautifully manifested my own.

Introduction

Once upon a time, a young kid in Hartford went away to become a Catholic priest. This departure was the beginning of a twelve-year journey. If there had been a parade when he entered the seminary as a thirteen-year-old boy, his Irish mother and father would have stood on the sidewalk applauding with the crowd. They were very proud and pleased, and his twin brother, relatives, and most of his friends would have been there too, also clapping and cheering. None of the proud spectators saw the gray clouds or the future rain coming that day. The clowns did, though. They were at the end of the procession and had stopped smiling. One of them had painted his face with bright blue circles around his eyes, a sad frown, and big red teardrops running down his cheeks. He tried to warn the unaware kid leading the parade about the impending storms. With all the shouting and cheers, no one heard that jester, and the rains came.

That young boy was me. My wife Donna, for many years, has encouraged me to write my story. She knows I have worn several different uniforms as I marched through my life's parade, and she finds some of them rather unique. She and many others have found it hard to believe I ever wore some of these outfits. A couple of those choices involved wearing a black suit with a white collar. I would later return that apparel to the empty closet of my former memories. I went to the law enforcement locker, where I found that my pants had a blue stripe, my shirt had a bright patch, and a place for a badge. I know everyone has fascinating accounts that fill their lives. I also realize my path has been unique as I have traveled through its various paths. The idea of sharing so many different experiences and feelings intrigues me. So many twists and turns have filled my life. I have lived a great deal of joy in a faith-filled life. I look forward to sharing some of those times. I have also known the experience of very personal sadness and hurt. These times are not easy for me to share. My priesthood ended when I finally had the courage and grace to admit my unhappiness as a celibate man. My days as a cop ended when I was almost killed on a rain-slicked road in a crushing cruiser accident. I have traveled many avenues since then.

We are all teachers. My road has been unique, but all of our streets are meaningful. I am confident I could also learn many important lessons from your experience. My life has been an exceptional classroom of happenings. The lessons I learned deny we merely exist in lives of "quiet desperation." Some would have us believe that. I do not, and I never have. We share thoughts about what faith, hope, and love mean in our lives. We face the reality of our mortality and question, like Alfie from long ago, "What's it all about?".

Chapter One: What's Past is Prologue

L ife is that wondrous world where we all stride in the landscape of our truth. We are all stories, open for review and recollection. You and I are the summations of those minutes passing in each specific hourglass that time our ways. Our years are the precious golden sands of each moment, falling until they fall no more. We search for meaning and an understanding of our paths. I am an old man who continues this quest. I know most of my days have passed. My hopes and dreams of another time are mostly memories. It is a regular occurrence for me now to get a phone call or text advising that some member of my family or friend has died. Thank God not too many. Several of my relatives and buddies now face severe illnesses. Some, once very athletic individuals, are now slowed by hearts that do not beat so well. Others, just recently healthy, now carry the dread of cancer or dementia that has stolen their memory and hope. I disagree with those self-assured folks who declare "aging is just a number." Perhaps their chocolate and peanut protein bars have made their later years easier. I sincerely hope so. Actually, "easy" has never described any of my former wanderings, and it does not define my present tense.

I have had some close calls with death and recall many who have gone before. I remember how my mother died when she was eighty-five years old. She suffered a severe stroke and was a patient at Hartford Hospital for several days. My brother and his wife had flown to Hartford from their home in Texas, and we discussed my mother's post-hospital care. Later, my wife and I visited her room on the fifth floor of the medical-surgical unit when my mom's condition worsened. She began to have short gasps and was having a hard time breathing. Donna rushed out to the nearby nurse's station and returned quickly. We held my mother's hand as a caring nurse tried to make her comfortable. I remember squeezing her hand and telling her, "Don't be afraid, mom. Donna and I are with you." She looked at me with one of the most peaceful gazes I have ever seen. She smiled and quietly said, "Chick, I'm not afraid." I tried to calm her, and she reassured me with the squeeze of her hand. Then she died.

I have been lucky with my health. I have no serious diseases, although I am a cancer survivor. I am forever grateful that my doctor, during my yearly experience of being poked and prodded, found an enlarged prostrate that was cancerous. This disease had not yet spread beyond the prostate gland, but tests indicated the compelling need for surgery. My operation took eleven hours. I remember waiting for my surgery, afraid and lying on a silver gurney pushed flat against the wall outside of the operating room. I thought of my wife, sitting in some waiting room, worried and nervous. What a kick. She was frightened for me, and I was anxious for her. I heard the banter of the nurses and doctors in the area, but I felt alone. I was freezing until someone put a warm, white blanket over me. A male orderly came out from behind the polished metal doors of the surgical suite and began wheeling me to the operating table. I whispered, "Here I am, Lord." I didn't know what else to pray or to say.

That talented surgeon and nursing staff saved my life. I do not take good health for granted, especially since I have been cancer-free for many years. I know my time is coming when the inevitable ailments of my age will overtake me. Older adults, like old cars, no matter how well-maintained, eventually start to break down. I wake every day with aches and pains, but I will still walk at least two miles today around the neighborhood I call home. There are woods nearby, and I love to go there and walk along the river. I go slower now, but I try to keep going. My only concern is the presence of brown bears who seem to like the same places.

My wife smiles as she likes to remind me that I now get out of bed much slower than in some former mornings. I catch her grin sometimes as she rolls over to grab some extra winks. She knows I am going to do the very same. I want you to know I still claim a full head of blond hair. I brag about this with my twin brother, Bill. His hair turned all white years ago. I finally must admit a few strands of that color are showing themselves in my morning mirror. I am not too pleased about that. Some truths just cannot be denied. I have tried to do that sometimes. I used to down Guinness on draft, followed by whiskey chasers, in what was another life. Those were years when two sixes were standard, and my dancing on a bar or a table was not unheard of, especially if "New York, New York" was playing. Goodbye to those good times. I still enjoy a nice glass of California Cabernet as I watch the eleven o'clock news, munching my whole wheat crackers and Swiss cheese.

My relationship with God, family, and friends has always been essential to me. I believe profoundly in a loving reality, way beyond my understanding, whom we mere humans call God. This conviction is intuitive to me. I cannot prove my faith with certainty. My whole life has been my attempt to live it. I am someone who loves deeply. I am aware that sometimes I do not love well. My Christian belief, and the beautiful dictates of so many other religions, invite the reality of love and forgiveness. There have been many times I have refused this invitation. This rejection is my definition of sin. The bright experience of hope also influences every moment of every day.

I believe there is sunshine after the darkest of storms. I have weathered those storms, sometimes with no protection against their howling winds. The warmth of a new day and another time have warmed my cold and chill. I prefer thinking the chalice of my life is at least half full. I share this belief because I have been that weary traveler who has known deep thirst in the wildernesses of my journey and has always found quenching drops of purpose to lead me on. My relationship with these realities has defined my history, and I value them immensely.

I know what alienation is and what it is like to be all alone. It was not a pleasant experience for me, and I will share those times with you. I also know what it is to be the center of everyone's attention.

That experience was pleasant for a bit, but it was lonely too. For some time, my life as a priest was like a circus. Those applauding spectators in the bleachers of the giant main tent did not see where the Ring Master went after exiting that center ring's spotlight. He lives in an old trailer near the hay for the horses and elephants. The area smells, and nobody walks there. That place beyond the crowd's view is lonely too. For a while, that ringmaster was me. My Barnum and Bailey world was the church, my parish was my arena, and I loved being the leading light that held the show together. I had few friendships with other performers, also known as priests. I seemed in total control when I walked around that bright center ring. I was not. Doubt and hurt lurked in the dimness beyond the bright light. I stood alone, basking in the attention, and I was lonely. I have spent my life trying to protect and serve all who came to the show. I was much happier as a cop than as a clergyman.

I look forward to sharing those days with you and the times that followed. I look forward to walking with you. I have been blessed with confidence that hides my self-doubt, a poise that can also be very solitary. My father was sometimes very critical of me, especially in my adolescent years. I was a kid, self-conscious about my horrible acne, and he occasionally called me painful names that carved scars into my memory. I know the awful hurt of judgment. This awareness began a long time ago for me. I grew up in a very loving home until it wasn't. After my father retired from the State Police, our home became a fear-filled, dysfunctional house for several years. I was about nine years old then. The violence of angry, loud shouts nurtured ugly weeds of fear, pain, shame, and guilt into the garden of my growth. My father's aggression cultivated my need to protect. My mother's sadness during that time galvanized my need to please and my desire to serve. I am pretty even-tempered, but I have little patience with drama and the people who foster it. Now you know why.

I love wearing nice suits and dressing up with crisp shirts and colorful ties. I have a frayed blue pinstriped suit that I still occasionally wear when going to the special occasions of my life,

4

like funerals and weddings. My day-to-day clothing choices include my wrangler jeans and a black t-shirt emblazoned with the Harley-Davidson motorcycle emblem. I like wearing various clothing styles, but I am a guy who is self-conscious about wearing a dress. I bet that sentence caught you off guard, just a bit. No, I wasn't showing up at parties in some slinky, bright-colored skirt. I never put on bobby sox or patent leather shoes, even in my wildest days. Back in my student days, though, I wore a cassock. This was a long black, full-length garment that clergy and seminarians wore as they went about their church rituals and duties. It was also a dress.

I studied for twelve long years, preparing for my life of ministry to the people of God. I began this education as a thirteen-year-old boy in an all-male high school called the "minor seminary." I didn't realize it then but entering that clerical training was my attempt to escape an unhappy family in a sincere but naïve effort to bring those loved ones some happiness. I was just a kid and knew nothing of life. I certainly understood little about my hopes and dreams. My goal was to please my parents, with little thought about pleasing myself. I would dedicate my life to God as a Catholic priest, and my mom and dad would live happily ever after.

Most of my classmates eventually decided against religious life and left the seminary before ordination. Some became teachers and social workers. Others went into the military. One, a U.S. Marine, died in the jungles of Viet Nam. They had all ended their studies before ordination, as my own continued. My education would ultimately take me to classrooms of colleges and universities all over the country, where I earned advanced degrees and certifications in theology and psychology. Still, my most crucial education took place in inner cities, hospital hallways, and the hollows of the Appalachian Mountains. My finest teachers were the people I met along those varied ways.

I was a priest for seven years and treasured the reward of helping people solve their problems and find meaning. I lived the contradiction of loving the good things I did for many people and disliking who I was when I was alone. I looked forward to those times after I finished my Sunday Mass when I spoke with the many people who had attended the service. Families shared plans for the day, and I envied them as they walked together to their cars. It was always a lonely ride for me back to the rectory. I never liked that drive. I wouldn't say I highly regarded wearing the black clerical suit either. I always felt I was on a pedestal and did not like standing there. Nothing I write here is an adverse judgment or criticism of many fine, humble, and loving priests who serve their people and their God. I have known some of them and loved the ministry we shared. The truth is that I eventually and finally realized that my vow of celibacy was not a blessing for me but a cross too heavy to bear. I finally acknowledged and admitted to myself that I was not a very happy man.

The sacred cloth of the Catholic Church has been torn by the scandal of pedophiles, monsters lurking behind the veil of holiness to destroy a child's trusting innocence. The reality of these monsters' disgusts and sickens me. I have met wonderful priests and nuns throughout my life. They live their lives in humility and dedication. Criminal investigations have indicated that some others I had studied with, lived with, or ministered with, were criminals. This amazes me since I was unaware or suspicious of their evil. I did not realize how many genuinely horrible people I counted as my brothers and sisters until the victims revealed their secrets. Eleven have been accused, and four have been arrested. I was shocked when their victims, innocent boys and girls, finally dared to speak up and make accusations. I still am. These clergy said their daily Mass and shared a variety of school classrooms and playgrounds. Their compassion at funerals for the grieving families appeared profound. Their prayers for the repose of those so many souls seemed sincere. They visited the sick and anointed them, and their prayers for eternal life were reverent. I shared meals with some of these experts at hiding and manipulation and seats at Red Sox baseball games with others. I feel for the church's many incredible men and women whose identities have been tainted by these others. I am also ashamed of those silent church leaders who never spoke up. I once considered that place home.

I changed my wardrobe when I left the priesthood. I traded the black suit of the clergy for a blue one and became a cop. I wore that uniform for 20 years. I loved being a cop. I know this sounds crazy, but I looked forward to working every day. I was a "street cop" who loved the call of my daily life to "protect and serve." The world of law enforcement is a military environment. The police department is a world run with discipline where time-honored rules and rigid regulations govern the behavior of those who have sworn to uphold the law. It seems that newspapers are daily filled with stories of racist cops, violent men, and women who dishonor their badges and oaths. I am sure they have been part of every police department's roll calls from the beginning of law enforcement. I thank God that their behaviors are no longer acceptable. I am also grateful I have not worked with them.

Prejudice in any form, racial, sexual, or religious, cannot be part of any police officer's mindset. It should never have been. I know courageous cops who put their lives on the line every shift. Others would rather stay away from the fray and not get involved when participation is demanded. I have known many cops, local, state, and federal. Most have been dedicated to being the best that they can be. There were a few who got tired of that effort. I know we all possess prejudice, in one form or another. We all have preconceived notions of one another based on our cultures and experience. Prejudice exists, but I know continuing education and increased diversity in the law enforcement world are lessening this reality in many police departments throughout our country. I am sure there are still racist cops who allow their feelings of power and arrogance to violate the rights of others. They disgrace the badge and have not been a part of my journey. Hopefully, better selection processes and training will keep these men and women from our streets. I do not want to forbid funding to our police departments. I want to prevent bad cops from ever walking those hallways. They have no place standing in "the long, blue line."

I agree with cops wearing cameras. There were none when I was on duty. I think their recordings provide an excellent positive witness for thousands of outstanding police officers and a blatant condemnation of those few who are not. I am sickened at the sight of police officers violating the rights of others. They dishonor the badge. Society is confronting them and holding them accountable. I am glad these few are found and arrested.

One of my father's favorite insights was that if a man wanted to "get along," he had to "go along." I don't know where he picked up that gem of wisdom, but I never bought into it. Perhaps he had a more subtle meaning. Maybe he meant that for me to get along with him, I had to go along with all he wanted. I have the sneaking suspicion that he wanted me to live up to all of his expectations, perhaps even his unmet wishes. I did not do that either. Maybe my father would have been a happier priest than I was. I do not know.

Before becoming a state trooper, and long before he met my mother, he had driven a bus for the Connecticut Company for a short time. He had great memories of those days driving between Hartford and Middletown. I fondly recall his smile as he sat on the edge of his bed in the nursing home and shared stories of the various passengers he had met. That grin broadened as he spoke of the pretty girls he used to flirt with. He surprised me with a comment shared a few weeks before he died. He told me he was proud of his career in the state police but would have preferred being a bus driver. I was shocked when he told me he did not like "worrying about other people." I have never been like that. I loved the experience of protecting and serving as a priest and a policeman. My journey has taught me a crucial conviction: I am called to love others as much as I love myself. I was not always so convinced. The sun sometimes hides in cloudy skies.

So here we are, sharing some thoughts as you are about to join me as I walk along my memory lane. Every new day brings more insights and learning. We do not even know one another, yet somehow, I want to share. I have finally come to that point along my road where I have wanted to be for a very long time. I know that this present time is such a critical moment for me. I hope my words remind you that your present tense is your most crucial time. Our pasts are gone with all their joys and sorrows. I cannot change my choices in so many of my yesterdays. There is so much I might have done differently had I known better. I did not. I can do nothing now but be a humble student and learn from those valued lessons, which I once called mistakes.

Our futures are not here, nor are they even promised for a moment. We all have plans, hopes, and dreams calling us from some tomorrow place. Life is very fragile, and often so little is within our control. The only reality that each one of us possesses is the present tense of our lives. I am sure you know, as well as me, that our lives do not promise another tomorrow. The older I have gotten, the more I have come to understand this. My search for meaning is why I am sharing these thoughts. It is time. I wish I could sit with you someplace, maybe in a little coffee shop, to share your thoughts and feelings about the roads you have walked. I can smell the aroma of some hot coffee brewing. I can hear the other patrons in their soft chairs enjoying the conversations making up their day and the quiet thoughts. I see some playing on their computer keyboards, waiting for another drink or more words. I would love to share with you and know that my journey and its lessons have meant something to you. That is why I write. I am a learner, though, and I would tell you that your own heart has so many lessons to teach. I invite you, in these words, to take the time for yourself, as I have, to stop for a moment and look at your paths and roadways. You may find that your journey, like mine, has brought you extraordinary moments.

My God has called me to share. This is my vocation. I think we all share this call. Perhaps, by learning a little bit about me, you might also find some lessons about yourself. These words are my attempt to follow my calling. I have written so many chapters in the book of my memories. I am an old man who hopefully has become wise with my years. That is my truth. I have tried to find my truth and God's will for me. Perhaps you can learn more about your truth as you read how I have discovered my own. I look out from these pages and across these sentences, black typed and stark on these pages, and I see you. I smile as I watch you reflect on your insights. I have had those same perceptions. I see them through the prism of my lifetime. I hope you find a deeper meaning in your life as you read about my own. I continue to find more profound truth, even as I write.

I hope I do not bore you with this recitation of me. I invite you to know me better. I want you to know my truth. Maybe you will learn a little more about your truth. You will meet people I have met but will not know by their names. I have changed most of those. You will travel to some of the places that I have gone. They are real. My memories of them are too. My perceptions are my truth as I try to paint pictures of a sometimes-blurred history. I hope you will understand some of my experiences within their different boundaries. Time has faded some of my yesterdays. The irony of memory is that it defines my past, my past that I no longer see. I have had the opportunity to make many choices in my long life. Many of them have been excellent and fill me with pride. I will tell you about some of them. Some decisions were abysmal and still caused me hurt. I will share those too. I know, finally, that I am worthwhile. I know, also, that you are too. I know, as well, that I am a very wounded healer. I always have been.

I now come to that place in the heart of my tarnished soul where two roads divide. I am an old man now. I am a man on a journey. My way is one of discovery and light. I do not choose the dark path of regret. I realize some walk this way. I know many of them. They look back on their yesterdays and wish they had lived other lives. They regret their memories. They ponder how their times might have been much better if they had made different decisions. I do not want to travel with them. I choose to be a mentor. I want to be an advisor who seeks to walk in the light. Welcome to my road. I hope you find your time here worth your while. My life has been a constant discovery by a sometimes-lost wanderer. I still search. In all these wanderings, I have learned to affirm who I am and who you are. I love sitting on an old park bench near a favorite lily pad pool. This area is my reflection place. I invite you to join me.

These reflections are my attempts at self-awareness as I walk along the horizon of my life. My morning mirror reflects a waking smile and my hair growing whiter and longer with every new day. I finally have something to share. My most fundamental identity is that I am a wounded healer. This definition is who I am. I am and always have been aware that my road always calls me to become more than I am. I want to share lessons I learned along the way with you throughout every day of every month of my life.

Chapter Two: The Way It Was

My story begins in Hartford, Connecticut, on July 13, 1947. It was an uneventful day, but it was not all silent. The various neighborhoods were all waking up like they always did as the sun began to show on what would be a warm and sunny day. Approximately 177,000 people lived in Hartford's various neighborhoods. Many different clans and cultures divided the city. The Irish and Italians in the south end of the town were having their early morning coffees. The smell of eggs frying and sausages wafted through the open windows in the close bordered homes with their small backyards. This area was a solidly middle-class neighborhood, and many would be leaving soon for their 7 am shifts at the huge Pratt and Whitney plant in East Hartford or maybe to jobs at the Royal Typewriter or Colt Firearms. Some mothers might be heading for the street corners to grab an early bus, taking them downtown to the Travelers Insurance company or one of the many other office buildings filled with the insurance business. Hartford was known as the "Insurance Capital of the World." Unemployment was low back then. Many families were beginning their day as mothers and fathers headed off to work. Back then, most families with cars had one car, and the driver was usually the man of the house. Only three people out of every hundred were not working at some job. The Second World War had ended two years previously. Many of these recently home veterans, like many others throughout the city, were happy to start their day with full stomachs and family sounds, reminding them that this would be a good day.

Two and three-family homes filled the North End. They were similar to those on many streets to the south of their neighborhoods. Some could afford to own their own single-family homes. There were crowded government-built housing projects in the center of all these streets. Stowe Village, Bowles Park, and Dutch Point were all coming awake. Charter Oak Terrace, in the south end, was also greeting the new day. These small residences gave hard-working people a chance at a better opportunity. Many had taken that chance. Hundreds of families of all cultural backgrounds and faiths, Black and White, lived together as friends. Jewish and African American neighborhoods in this area shared much about their common understanding of racial hatred and the need for communal protection. Many would recall that time as a good time. Their homes were not the filthy, rat-infested, rundown places they would someday become. Jewish and African American families were beginning their day as well.

Many neighborhood minority-owned grocery stores were opening their doors to the new dawn. Cash registers were beginning to chime with the purchases of freshly brewed coffee. The newly wiped counters displayed the morning editions of the *Hartford Courant*. Many this day were walking into the Jewish bakeries too. Mothers, fathers, uncles, aunts, and grandparents had been hard at work since 3 am, making the wonderful smelling dark loaves of bread and creating the cream and red-filled jelly donuts that would soon fill lunch boxes and breakfast plates. Newspaper delivery boys enjoyed the warm, freshly made honey-dipped donuts, saved for them by a happy baker eager to read about Yogi Berra. This day would become another regular date on the calendar for most people as life continued.

Many French-speaking families had streamed into the city for factory work. The war had made many refugees, and some from Europe and Canada rushed to the Royal Typewriter factory, just a mile from their apartments, tenements, and tiny homes, many of which had been home to other immigrants in other times of global crisis. This business was a place where hundreds of their French-speaking brothers and sisters were already employed. There was a beautiful park nearby, Pope Park. These ninety acres of flowers and greenery were a welcome space for many whose homes had neither flowers nor foliage decorating any part of their place. It had been donated by and named after Col. Augustus Pope, who had become rich in manufacturing bicycles and motor vehicles at the turn of the century. Residents here began their day, like so many others in the various neighborhoods, kissing their children goodbye and heading out into Frog Hollow, which residents called their community. July 13, 1947, was a Sunday. Catholic families were getting ready to go to Mass all over the city. Other families would be joining their various congregations to share in Bible readings by their ministers and beautiful spirituals. Jewish families had already celebrated their Sabbath the previous day, and now their Sunday sports pages and comics were opening to the latest news of the Yankees or what was happening in Dick Tracy's life.

LIFE magazine had just come out with another issue. Many in Harford would be paging through its contents, enjoying the stories of other lives in other places. The cover, that July, was a color photograph of a smiling little girl in a light blue dress. She had a broad smile and joyfully held on to a galloping wooden horse on a whirling music-filled merry-go-round. The horse was white and had golden hoofs galloping to some imaginary destination. The joyful rider was balanced and precarious on a saddle painted with the American flag. The photo proclaimed for all to see that life was good in this pleasant land. Some businessmen and wealthy travelers drove away from Hartford to Bradley Airport, named after a deceased Air Force pilot killed in a crash during a training mission. This hub of activity had recently opened to civilian passengers. Many travelers were looking forward to their flights on this sunny July day.

My father was a CT. State Trooper, and he was working the midnight shift. His radio call sign was KCH 788, stationed at Troop H in Hartford. He had been on duty since 11p.m. the previous night and had spent the dark hours patrolling the Berlin Turnpike, a significant roadway known as Route 5/15. This road had been built in 1798 and was a toll road initially built to connect Hartford and New Haven. It continued that route and was a very well-traveled road, filled with cars and trucks heading south, in 1947, south to

New York or north to Boston. My father was anticipating the end of his shift at 7 a.m. and looking forward to returning to St. Francis Hospital. He had been there the night before, as my mom had gone there 16 hours previously, with labor pains. At 3:15, my father's shift came to an abrupt end. The Troop H dispatcher had advised him to head for St. Francis Hospital. The Shift Supervisor took to the radio and congratulated him that he was a new father. Five minutes later, State Police dispatch again breached the airways with the news of a new son. The dispatcher replied with the information that there were now two sons, not one. I entered this world at 3:00 am. My brother followed at 3:05. I laughed and smiled at the story of my father's response to this news as he headed for the hospital. Some of his friends from that time swear that his radio went silent. This day was pretty uneventful for everyone except for my brother and me. On July 13, 1947, we were the main event.

The absolute irony of my life is that I have many "once upon a time" roads in my zig-zag journey. This time, right now, is a horrible moment in history for all of us. People are dying from a horrendous pandemic from a virus called Corona. There is so much fear and suspicion all around us, fostered by a fractured political system and changing demography in our country. We have spent months walking around with masks covering our faces as we looked into each other's eyes, wondering how we all would be. Daily we have listened to the newscasters as they spoke from their homes, too concerned and wary of their television stations, as they shared with us the numbers of newly infected and newly dead. A horrible war rages in Ukraine, where Russian soldiers slaughter innocents as I type these words.

I know I have fewer days ahead of me than those I leave behind. According to the U.S. Center for Disease Control, I can expect to live until I am 75.1 years old. My time is flying by. This reality has made my present tense so much more important than it might have been. I appreciate moments and memories much more than I once did. I recently shared with my daughter, Marci, that I envied her and her future days. I did not say this with regret, just acknowledgment of the truth. Time is limited. Lately, I have come to understand that much of my life has now passed, and I have wasted many moments on negative thoughts and hurtful experiences. I have heard others sometimes say they have no regrets. I envy them. Many wrong turns and missteps fill my journey. You also need to know that I spent years of my life lost in a wilderness of hurt and doubt. I have often reflected on the reality that my life has been a journey. I have often been lost in the woods of distrust and hurt. I know the experience of being selfish deeply. This choice is my definition of sin, and I know I am a sinful man. I also see the background of grace-filled love in my understanding of God. I know I am faith-filled as well.

I can't entirely agree with those who say it makes no sense to reflect on negatives in the past. They are my lessons. I have learned from those steps, which have brought me to this day and the insights I share. I sincerely believe that I have made many mistakes in my life, where I have hurt others because of my selfishness. Maybe mistake is not the correct word to describe soul-wrenching times along my way. I have made many poor decisions, some with the best intentions. They have become my lessons and my soul knowledge of myself and God. They have become my signpost along my many roads, directing me away from toxic experiences and toxic people. I want to share this map with you as well. These pandemic times have focused those moments like a laser for me. People are dying. I want to live.

Chapter Three: Once Upon A Time

O nce upon a time is how so many children's stories seem to begin. Many of them have interesting, memorable characters reaching out to us from all their pages, who can teach us some precious lessons, or maybe ones not so special. Most of us remember these tales from our varied childhoods. Once upon a time, a little girl who wore a red riding hood went to her grandmother's house. Once upon another time, there was a giant who bellowed out loudly about the blood of some Englishman. Another yarn tells us that once there was a beautiful princess with a glass shoe, and also smiles with an arrogant rabbit who laughed at a slow-moving tortoise.

I did not grow up in a home where I heard many fairy tales or make-believe stories. Perhaps that is why, as an adult, I love to share stories, especially with young kids. I remember, as a college seminarian, sharing the exploits of Captain Kid with the orphans at St. Colman's in Watervliet, NY. I have lovely memories of attending the grade school adjacent to the church and reading to the first and second graders as a young priest at St. Joseph's, in a parish outside of Boston. Even as a cop, many years later, I would sometimes stop at the local nursery school at the Congregational church and regale the kids with stories of green dragons and knights in their shining armor. One of my favorite personal photographs is a picture of myself and one of my granddaughters sitting in the living room of the log house I once owned. It's an old photo now, bent and folded with age. My wife took the photo twenty-five years ago. My granddaughter is five years old, and I might have been considered young, maybe in my early forties. I am reading to her from a dog-eared book that she carried everywhere. She sits next to me, looking up at me with eyes rapt and her face filled with wonder and attention. I don't remember the story I was reading. I know there are no such photos from my childhood of any such storytelling or wide-eyed wonder.

I never heard any childhood stories from my father. My brother and I never had the experience of sitting on the floor listening to him read from his overstuffed chair about some fire-belching dragon, a pretty princess, or even a bunny rabbit hopping down some trail. He had no stories of his childhood either. I never heard him speak of his father. I do not recall my father ever speaking about any of his family. Over the years, I have enjoyed sharing my own childhood experiences. I have shared many positive and negative memories with friends and relatives. They have also shared with me. I have found bits of wisdom and grace that remain with me in these stories. It seems to me that this sharing is an essential fabric in the tapestry of my history. I regret that I never learned more about those times in my parent's childhood during my childhood. I would find out many years later that he had a brother named Frank, who died due to brain cancer while raising a young family in Middletown, CT.

My brother has an ancient bible that sat unopened in our home as kids. In the fifties, people who read bibles were probably Protestant. They did a lot of bible reading. Bible reading was not the choice for an Irish Catholic family. I think my father relegated these holy scriptures to our cellar. They found their resting spot there, along with the paint cans and tarps for hauling the backyard leaves. There was an old roll-top desk down there, and I somehow recall seeing that Holy Bible, dusty and unread, somewhere on that desk. At the beginning of that holy book was the information about the Baptism ceremony for a sister my father had. She must have died as a little girl. There was never any mention of her. My mother's only comment about my father's family was that they were "lovely" people. I have heard that he grew up in an upper-middle-class family. His childhood was during the great depression of the late1920s. Many others were living in poverty, but my father could still study music and have a piano in his boyhood home.

I know nothing about my grandparents except that, according to my mother, my maternal grandmother was very Irish, demanding, and selfish. She saw herself as a martyr, which is exactly how my mother came to see herself. Maybe they were both right. I am sure my parents loved my brother and me very much, although I have no memory of many hugs from either one of them. Affection for us was real, but very seldom physically expressed. I do remember sometime smiles and loving looks towards us. They spoke with little or no love towards one another. I know I never saw them holding hands. There is a black and white photo from their dating days, where they seem very happy and in love. I think they loved one another, just like what was so apparent in that happy photo. That love was so imperfect and with so much dysfunction. My lifetime of trying to love is a reflection of all of those times. I know there were sometimes days filled with smiles, laughter, and genuine care. There were also tears. My own life for many years would reflect those days.

The Goodwin Public Library was my childhood place for many of these lessons. Often it became a special place for my brother and me. It was not a very impressive building. There were story hours read to children on many rainy Saturday afternoons. This location was where a fantastic tale became authentic and exciting to neighborhood kids. Sometimes this was where we went when my father told us not to come home until supper time, which meant to stay away.

Looking back now, I smile. It was only one story, and after walking into the entrance, I remember walking by the main counter and two large rooms. The room on the left was for the grown-up books. The center area had a section for magazines. The room to the right was where, for those of you old enough to remember, the Hardy boys lived there amidst the 101 Dalmatians and maybe a little girl named Charlotte who was weaving a unique web. The true stories about our favorite sports figures, like Babe Ruth and Jimmy Piersall, were on polished wooden shelves closer to the magazine section, well within the view of Mrs. Woodward, one of my favorite people. She ruled this location as if it were her kingdom. She was probably in her forties. Wow, how young that seems to me now. She seemed ancient to me, all of nine or ten years old myself. I thought she was one of the most intelligent people I had ever met, and the library seemed to be her home. She was always there. Her glasses didn't have any frames, and as she looked over the rims, watching the goings-on of her world, there was an air of authority that no adult or child ever questioned. She was a short lady but her heavier weight added to her dimensions. She enforced a rule of silence in that place. I think that's why it became such an occasional haven for me. There was not a lot of silence in my home.

My mother and father loved my brother and me. I never doubted that even after what would happen to our relationships many years later. My mother's affection was shown much more in her actions than in her words. My earliest memories of my mother are collages of smiles, laughter, and sometimes tears. Her smile was all-encompassing to her life and mine. Her tears would become that way too. One of my favorite memories of those years, so long ago, is of her walking with my brother and me, as little boys of maybe five or six years old, to Elizabeth Park in Hartford. It was a two-mile walk from our three-family home on South Whitney Street. I remember we would pass the firehouse, Engine 12, just up the street from where we lived.

Sometimes, the firefighters would stand out in front of the doors where the two fire trucks parked. They always waved to us and sometimes invited us to see the big red trucks they would be racing into the street sometimes during the day. They had a mascot, a white Dalmatian dog with a black-spotted coat. He was always friendly, and I loved when we could run over to greet him. Then it was off to Goursin's, the corner drug store on Farmington Avenue, where my brother and I often feasted on ice cream cones or candy. I smile at those times. They are happy memories for me.

One of my favorite places at the park was where the monkey bars were. These were a scrambled assembly of pipes going up and down and all directions, and I loved to climb them. My brother and

I would chase each other around this conglomeration of steel until the near-by swings beckoned us. I heard my mother's laughter as she pushed us higher and higher until I felt I might almost fly. It was essential for her that we have fun. I still hear her laughter as my brother and I chased each other around the ponds and playgrounds of those sunny days. This wonderful area also had a beautiful garden filled with hundreds of multicolored rose bushes.

There were green and brown painted park benches near these flowers. My mother sometimes sat there as we kids enjoyed our time running around this flower-filled place. Perhaps she found her peace during those visits to the park. It is ironic, but I still go to those same gardens and sit on maybe some of those same benches from those days so long ago. It is one of the places where I find my peace as well. Occasionally, some happy memories peek out from the fabric of my childhood, from those days of running so free from care. My mother was not very well versed in the words of many fairy tale times. She was much more versed in telling us about her sad childhood and her demanding Irish mother. She was very well-versed in taking care of her twins. They were her life, even with all the sadness she lived or would live from those days. I do not recall her saying "I love you" very often. I know she did live those words.

When I grew up, we did not have a family car. I do not recall any families in our neighborhood having two cars. We rode the public buses a lot, or we walked. My father was a state policeman, so our car was his police cruiser. My mother often took the bus to work at the New England Telephone Company, where she worked as a telephone operator. We would sometimes wait for my mother at the New Britain Avenue bus stop after coming home from work. I remember a purse snatching where a drunk had pushed a woman to the ground during a robbery. We worried about her. I do not recall two little boys saying "I love you" very often to their mother. I know that, like her, we lived those words, even as little boys. Even then, I was becoming a protector.

I remember when I was a young priest struggling to remain faithful and faith filled. I felt that somewhere in the shadows of those times, there were lessons to be learned. I was arrogant enough back then to think that it might be worth my while and yours for me to share them. It seems like I have wanted to write these words for years. Maybe today, finally, I have reached a level of humility that maybe, just perhaps, there are lessons to be learned that we all can teach. These pages may contain some meaning for you, which may help or cause you to smile or reflect. I have always felt a deep need to help others, even as a young boy coming to my mother's defense in a sometimes very abusive household. Looking back on all of those early years that led to my becoming a priest, I know that my path was one that often walked in the sunlight, sometimes in the shadows, and there were blistering cold and stormy nights. I believe that God calls us to serve one another. I also understand that He calls us to love ourselves in the deepest parts of my soul. This realization would ultimately lead me away from the priesthood and Catholic church to a profession wearing a badge and a 9-millimeter gun, a far cry from a cross and a white collar. A large truck crashing into my police car ended this career. I would later be elected to public office, substitute in a high school classroom, and own a business. I ultimately walked along the corporate halls of a large personal injury law firm, where I taught about communication and learned new marketing and public relations insights daily.

I have discovered a great deal along my way through my various paths. I know God has called me to be a healer throughout my life and with my own words. I am not foolish to think that this calling reflects my remarkable life. My primary definition of myself is that of a wounded healer. My selfishness has hurt others. My sinfulness has caused me to know the experience of "Oh my God, I am heartily sorry." I wrote that prayer of my youth on my soul, and they are not just words for me. A song from many years ago reflects on the singer's life and many descriptions of his reality. I echo that in mine. I am a poet, not a piper. I know what it means to be down and out emotionally, spiritually, and in my living reality. I know what it is like to be poor financially, spiritually, and emotionally.

I had to borrow a car once upon a time because I could not afford my own. I once lived in a rented room because I could not afford an apartment, even a cheap one. My first job after I left the priesthood was as a security officer. I wore a gray uniform with a shirt too big and pants that I could hardly button. I walked around a dark, empty factory checking windows and doors for minimum wage. I might have been homeless too, but for the kindness of one family who had befriended me. I have never been a king, but I have held elected office and helped lead the governance of thousands of people. I have been a teacher but, more importantly, a constant learner; these words now reflect some of those lessons.

Tears have sometimes instructed my heart, fears, hopes, and joy. I am a man of faith. I also listen to God's voice in the silence of my being. My prayer is the prayer of St. Paul. "Lord, I believe, help my unbelief." The most important story from the Old Testament is when God tells Moses, in the voice from a burning bush, "Go down and tell my people that I AM. They do not need to know my name." The Israelites had been wandering so lost through their desert for many years. They were hungry and poor and tattered and losing hope. I am paraphrasing now, but God told Moses, "Get down from this mountain and tell that stubborn gathering out there, stumbling amongst the locusts and dry sands, that I am their God, and they are my people." That reassurance was indeed enough for them. It has certainly been enough for me.

Chapter Four: Not Many Fairy Tales

I need to write because I need to understand. I need to put down these words because I am somehow a constant learner. I learn in the reflection of these sentences. I am the smiling kid in the not-all-the-time innocent kindergarten of my life's school. I smile as I try to figure out from this vantage place of old just what grade I might be in, walking through the halls of my heart's academia. I smile, thinking that I might have skipped a few steps. Perhaps I could have and should have repeated a few as well. I do know that I need to share whatever learning I may have garnered from those seminars with my searching soul.

My lessons are my truth. These sentences are my attempt to tell my fact to you. I am an artist, and my words are my canvas. I am somehow an illustrator, creating a reality of words with many impressionistic colors, some bright blue and red, against the backdrop of sometimes gray and mellow brown. I understand that this present moment, this brushstroke of me, is my most crucial moment. I have no tomorrow promised to me. Every one of my yesterdays is no longer. I can do nothing about them except make choices about learning, becoming, and doing. I want somehow to be extraordinary, even in my most ordinary time. I wish that for you as well. Our times fill each of us with choice and possibility. I realize that all I can do is listen to my voice, the self who shares my purpose with me. This moment is one of remembrance for me and a possibility. I have sometimes been an imperfect pilgrim in all my wanderings. I still am.

I know in the deepest part of my soul that my God has called me always to be more, even as He accepts me exactly as I am. I have not always responded to that call or fully understood it. My history fills my days with many turns along my way: my tears, fears, joys and laughter, contradictions, and the myriads of people who have peopled my journey. Truth is the only accurate compass for any of us as we walk our ways. My truth has been the compass of my goodness. I lost my way when I have been most dishonest with myself, with others, and with my God. We lie to ourselves when we are arrogant instead of humble when we put others down instead of building them up. We lie to get "our" way instead of what we know is the right way. The moral choice often means more effort or sacrifice and more love and forgiveness. I have found that lies are the coward's way. It takes much more courage to be honest with ourselves and others, and so I write. My days are becoming shorter now, as my future calls me into an even shorter winter. I have had a life filled with so much and devoid of so much. I have known saints in guttered ways, as they cared for one another in the rain, cold, and poverty that poured on their lives. I have known sinners too. I recognized them by their harsh judgments of others and the arrogance of their supposed holiness. I have lived in both grace and sin. Beyond all other definitions of my life, I know that I am a wounded healer.

I have spent many months wondering what my wife might do if I died during the pandemic. Or horrible to ponder what I might do if she passed. I thought of my daughter and the kaleidoscope of emotions I have faced, just worrying about her and her future. I have learned some things along the way during my many years. This present time is my teacher. It tells me in a whisper or sometimes a booming shout from the quiet hills around my home that this present moment is my only time. Most of what were once my tomorrows are now over, and hopefully, many of yours are yet to come. Countless of my dreams are now my memories. I weave them with a fragile thread that has been a regular part of the fabric of my life. Truth is always better than deceit. Success is always better than failure. Being my best has always been better than settling for being less than I know I could be. Through a lot of hurt, pain, tears, and fears, I have learned that you and I are here for the same reason.

Life calls us to be the very best persons that we can be

This beckoning means choosing what is correct instead of easy or popular. Sometimes reality whispers to us to speak out when others are quiet. In both of these situations, I have occasionally failed miserably. Realizing this, I try not to judge others. I know this is not always easy. I have found it is much easier to criticize than to understand. I have also learned that forgiving myself allows me never to give up and helps me forgive others. I know in my heart that it is all right to be imperfect. As my heart beats, I also know it is not all right to settle for imperfection. It never is. Personal excellence is not an easy calling. I know that often I was far from an ideal son. I misinterpreted advice as criticism and discipline as dislike. These realities were all based on love. Sometimes, I was too self-centered to see this. I ask you, from my vantage point of so many years and tears in my own heart, do not settle for being less than you can be. Listen to my whisper through these pages.

Being a good person is much more important than being liked. It is much more important to be proud because you have done your best than to be satisfied with doing less. It is a blessing to be beautiful on the "outside." The challenge for us is to be beautiful on the "inside." My mom and dad were far from perfect, just like me and you, and everyone else for that matter, who walks along on this earth. They knew more than me, though, and I had difficulty admitting their wisdom was at least as valid as my insufficient knowledge. They did their best, lived, and told the truth as they knew it. I have known for a very long time that none of us is perfect. I am convinced that the most crucial reality of love is being able to forgive, beginning with myself and then with you. I get up after a fall and try again to improve. Failure can never be an excuse to give up trying. I chose to get up every time I fell. I decided to keep on keeping on. Our lives are like gardens. They can have beautiful rainbow-colored flowers of love and forgiveness for ourselves and those others who bless our lives and are far from perfect. These bouquets of meaning are grown in the dark earth of effort and sacrifice, laughter and joy. The dirty weeds of selfishness, laziness, anger, dishonesty, lies, criticism, and pain prevent that growth. I have come to understand that how we bloom is up to each one of us. It is all up to you. I invite you to never settle for being anyone less than your best. This maturity is not easy. I know this very, very well, from my own experience along my way through all my many years. Every day of our lives calls us to become more with every new day. I do believe that God does not make junk! It is now time for me to write of my pilgrimage. It is finally time for me to share my "once upon a time."

Chapter Five: I Need to Write

The calling to love others is my best answer to the question of my search for meaning. I try to live this commitment, often very poorly. Ultimately, though, it is the reality of my definition of me. My self-awareness tells me I need to be for someone other than myself daily. This is why I write. Everything I have pondered in my studies of psychology and theology, even my understanding of history and literature, all tell me that a meaningful life must be a loving life. I realize very well that I have lived very selfish moments. There have been times when I have preferred pride to humility and self-interest to self-sacrifice. Those occasions were all about just myself, and I was not happy. Life has not been good for me during those instances of selfishness. I am convinced that I must decide every day to say "yes" to those in my life who so beautifully say "yes" to me. I also have to affirm those who do not.

This experience of respect and acknowledgment is where my faith comes in. I believe that my life is a reflection of God's presence in my world. I only have a small space where I walk, but I am dedicated to filling my world with whatever joy and forgiveness I can bring. My God loves without condition, accepts without constraint, and forgives without need. That is what I have tried. I have mostly failed in these efforts, although I continue my feeble efforts. I know that this is what my Creator calls me to do. I have not always been a perfect husband or father. I am aware of those times when I have let my wife and daughter down. I have found that my family is the best place for me to love and be loved. My home is that exceptional place where my God calls me to say "yes" to others, without condition, so I can also say "yes" to myself. For me, this is the essence of what love is all about. It is my definition of grace.

I have had a unique life journey as a priest, teacher, therapist, police officer, politician, entrepreneur, and businessman. These all share the very real and deep common denominator of service. I define my personal success by how much I have helped others. I have gotten tremendous satisfaction when I have done this well. I have also known the deep frustration of disappointment when I have not. This effort requires, again, the decision to go above and beyond my feelings. There have been moments when I have not felt like caring. There have been times when hurt feelings have stopped me in my tracks. I know that the journey toward goodness always demands a commitment to others. Every day, it is a decision that requires my mind, heart, and soul to live in love and forgiveness. This choice is my daily mission toward fulfillment. It is also why I write.

I am finally a journeyed soul. I am a wounded man who has sought my imperfect way to heal myself and others. I know that my wholeness and my own holiness are synonymous. I have tried to become more whole and, therefore, more holy. I do not think sad saints exist, although many have experienced unhappy times. I think all of our lives are efforts towards some sense of joy and peace. These observations are some of my reflections on those attempts.

I know that the horrible time of Corona disease and pandemic is finally coming to an end. The whole world has faced a new wave of disease and death, which, at long last, has come under control. Even as I write these words, mask mandates have finally wound down, as life-saving vaccines became more produced and shared. I have gotten my two shots of the Pfizer vaccine and the boosters. After I received my shots, I remember feeling freedom and a sense of relief that I had not experienced for a long time. I am now far less worried about physical contact with my family and friends. I love hugs and handshakes. I need closeness. Actually, I thrive on it. There was a time in my life when I was estranged from my mother and father. Every day, during that period, was shaded in sadness. Three years later, there was reconciliation and forgiveness, on my part and theirs, and a contact that would remain close for the rest of their lives. Distance, whether emotional or physical, is life-denying and joy-stealing. The personal touch is so important to all of us, and finally, we are no longer separated by the suggestions of distance and isolation, that the pandemic demanded. Authorities throughout our country and our world are inviting normalcy again. Kids are outside playing now and I am back to the ballfields watching my grandchildren play their sports. Distance between us is disappearing, and I am glad.

Elizabeth Park is a city park located in Hartford, about seven miles from my home, and I love to walk there. It is a quiet place and my soul listens best in solitude. There are over a hundred acres of walking trails, beautiful rose gardens, and shaded quiet places where I love to sit and breathe in my reality. I am thrilled that other people have returned to this beauty. I enjoy walking by a young couple when they turn towards me and share a smile or a friendly wave. Even with the memory of so much recent disruption in our lives, life is back to normal. I know that just as the many colored red and yellow tulips and roses bloom and return every year, despite the wintered storms and frost, so has the health of our world. There is always a rainbow after the storm. There are the blue skies of healing and the sunshine of a cure. This knowledge is a blessing to me.

These years of social quarantine that we all experienced have been very difficult for me. I have not lost anyone to this pandemic, although many of my family and friends have been sick. I can only imagine what those myriads of sad people, who have lost loved ones, must have experienced. The many pictures of weeping families who said goodbye to dying relatives on a distant iPad are unforgettable memories for me. I remember seeing a photo of a little girl waving through a window to her very ill grandmother, lying motionless in a nursing home bed, attached to a ventilator that soon will not be needed. I wondered if that dying loved one knew of her weeping granddaughter's presence and loving care. Those days of so much death are finally past. I understand the tears of nurses frustrated at the horrible experience of an intubated patient who will never say goodbye to a child. Medical staff will forever wash those times in their remembrance of sadness and frustration. We have been kept away from one another for months. This distance has affected me. I do not mind being alone, but loneliness negatively affects me. I had many reasons for my decision to leave the Catholic clergy. I think this sense of remoteness was the ultimate reason I left the priesthood. I needed a unique closeness not possible within the boundaries of a celibate lifestyle. I have learned many lessons along my way. These tumultuous days of pandemics have reinforced the magic and importance of appreciating the moment. I do not take tomorrow for granted. Life has always been too fragile for that.

These terrible times of pandemics have reinforced my deep belief that even the most superficial experiences shared with my wife, daughter, grandchildren, and friends fill me with meaning. Moments of laughter, smiles, forgiveness, and touch have meant so much. This fragility reminds me how precious our lives are to one another and ourselves. Taking advantage of these experiences has been a blessing to me as I reflect on all of my yesterdays.

I know that my glass is half full. I did not grow up in a storybook childhood, yet somehow my memories of the good outweigh the bad. Yet many of those recollections are tear flecked. I spent my young adult years as a Catholic priest experiencing many doubts about my faith and future. I never doubted who I was. Later on, I was almost killed as a police officer and went into a profound depression when I found, after months of physical therapy, that I would no longer be able to protect and serve. Again, somehow, I did not doubt who I was, even as a future unknown to me beckoned me to an unfamiliar tomorrow. Many years later, after hearing the frightening diagnosis of prostate cancer, my mortality hit me square in my soul. I remember weeping in the doctor's office after his words of explanation about what my possible options might be. I cannot imagine what the toll must be like for a surgeon to inform people on a daily basis that a terrible enemy had invaded their bodies and wanted to kill them. This specialist did so with a certainty and kindness which was both dire and reassuring at the same time. Somehow, still, I did not doubt that I could beat this cancer reality, too, as I had done with so many other dark times in my life. I have come to understand that the reality of change is an absolute in my life. My life is different every day, and accepting that fact is critical for me. My attitude towards that certitude determines my possibility. I am a very realistic optimist. This personal worldview has been my life's defining sentence.

I know that a sense of optimism is much more critical and valuable than any sense of dread. There have been days in my life filled with storms and the promise of darkening clouds. Existential rains have drenched me. I also know they sometimes saturate all of our daily lives. I have somehow been able to keep going forward. The muddy roads of fear and the slippery walks of doubt made this effort almost impossible, but I know I always kept going. I am a guy who is an optimist. I believe in rainbows and their cheerful colors promising better days. I know that at some point, the thundering storm will end. I also know at some point the darkness will inevitably become light. There were times when I had no idea what the implications of that sentence might be. I realize though, that I have a beautiful wife, a wonderful daughter, a cherished twin brother, and a valued family. I also have incredible friends who stay "in touch" regularly. I have decided to make time, every day, to do the same for them. All of these people make sure I know I am cared for and loved. I try to make sure that they are, too, moment to moment sometimes.

I know that effort and work are involved in finding meaning where there seems to be none. I am not a passive participant in existence. It seems to me that there are way too many of these people already. I do not want to walk with them. I have never been a part of their community. I am a proactive player in the game of my life. I am sometimes astonished by the pleasant surprises that life brings to me. I still find my existence breathtaking, even when confusing and perplexing. I do not let negative thoughts or feelings stay forever in my consciousness. I avoid negative people as much as I can. I have wasted too many hours of my limited time with them. I avoid negative experiences as well. I already had too many of those.

"Yes, I can" are the governing words of my life. This sentence has been my proclamation, even when it was only a silent prayer of hope and faith. "I can't" is a contradiction for me. It is a personal heresy. It is a denial of my faith in myself and God, whose words I sincerely believe. I know that there is enough darkness all around. There always has been. I am very aware of our world's darkness, and the shadows which have lived in my life, but I am a light seeker. I am far from a perfect man, but I am trying to be a candle in the occasional storms that pass through my days. I have come to appreciate self-acceptance and affirmation in new and more profound ways. This renewed understanding has been a blessing to me. I hope you will also find the grace of hope and life enthusiasm in these words. I want to be a light bearer for you.

I was confused about a lot during my adolescent years. You probably realize that by now. The idea of the Catholic priesthood was very appealing to me when I was fourteen years old. My Uncle was a priest. We called him Fr. Ed. I envied his lifestyle and his place on the cultural ladder of our Irish Catholic culture. Everyone I knew looked up to him. Doctors and lawyers even admired him. On some level, that admiration was very appealing to me. I also saw how my mother and father held him in awe. That might not be such a wrong place to live. I was so innocent of so much and so unknowing. I loved the idea that everyone looked at me in eighth grade at Holy Trinity Catholic school with a new sense of admiration. Sister Anna used me as an example of excellence, whereas once upon a time, I was a consistent challenge. I remember that I was not one of her favorites until I shared my desire to become a priest. Looking back, I find it amazing that anyone, especially me, could have considered such a life-altering calling with so little life experience. I think that my going into the high school seminary was my way of running away from my home. Somehow, I was on a pedestal and liked the admiration I felt in my small Catholic world. I also hoped I was living up to my parent's expectations of me. I realized that I had no clue at that time about my own. My calling was not to become a priest but to live up to the expectations of my Irish parents. I searched for so many years to find my own identity. I would discover that my personhood demanded that I find my expectations. The deep need for intimacy kept nagging at my existence, reminding me that I needed to be courageous with my choices or choose to be a coward before my God and myself. I thought I had so many answers back then. I did not.

My wife recently showed me a photograph taken at my first Mass. I was standing there with seven other priests, one of whom was my uncle, Fr. Ed. He was a priest and had been my idol and idea of manhood for many years. In the picture, I was raising the host as my brother priests and I prepared to share communion. We wore beautifully embroidered vestments, and a fine mist of scented incense rose from the altar, carrying our prayers to the Jesus I now represented at that altar. I looked out over the congregation of over 1200 people, most of whom were my family and friends. Looking at that picture, after all these many years, I remembered the tremendous sense of happiness I felt at that moment. I looked at my beaming parents seated in the first row of those pews at St. Lawrence O'Toole church. My mother and father were pleased beyond description. I was happy too, more for them, though, not myself. I distinctly remember having a deep sense of gnawing doubt at the moment that picture brings to life. This uncertainty would become a rock-solid conviction that perhaps I should never have stood at this altar.

I would be a priest for seven years and later a police officer for 20 more. After that, there would be many other paths which I would walk. I owned many different job titles and lived many other descriptions. I would be a teacher, a psychotherapist, a public speaker, an entrepreneur, a politician, and a businessman. Everything I have done is a reflection of who I am. Ultimately though, these final years of my journey have been spent just trying to be a humble man for those whom God has placed in my life. I do not have the specific answers to their sometimes difficult questions about their own trinity of past, present, and future. They have their own paths to walk. I know, though, that I am perhaps a man who finally has gained some wisdom that might be worthwhile to share with them and with you. I hope so.

Personal definitions fill your life and mine. They not only fill our lives in our present moments. They have been part of our history from our earliest days. I have found that I do this to myself. At various times I am an optimist. Sometimes, I speak to myself of my realism or smile at the sense of humor that sometimes peeks into my meaning of me. I have also discovered, get ready for this, the genuine truth that others are often pleased to define us. I know you will find this hard to believe, but sometimes those definitions are negative. "What an asshole!" "What an idiot!" What a kick!

Ultimately though, we are all special editions of unique histories. We each have our distinctive chapter in our singular volume. A few of us have gold embossed covers, leather, and expensive and very special. These sit unread and unknown in the dusty recesses of some imagined repository. They stay on their protected shelves in their quiet libraries of reality. Fragile pages keep them from being seen or even opened by many. Other volumes are much more well-read. Many have viewed their pages, some worn and tattered by use and maybe age too. Other exciting works have found space for the chapters of their binding. They are in plain view, more protected on higher shelves by more watchful eyes. They are viewed and appreciated for their beauty as well as their content. There are not many of these. Perhaps, that is why they are so valued, even by the infrequent visitor to these displays of lifetimes and memories. More important, though, these works are appreciated and valued.

I have been like those very special folios, sometimes hidden from view and protected on the shelves of my soul. There have been different times when the pages of my chapters have been bent and torn. They seemed like a tattered, worn paperback dropped on the side of a well-traveled road. I know that you and I are unique creations, no matter the condition of our bindings or pages. This conviction lives strong in my life. Each one of us is a special edition of meaning and understanding. The many diverse dust jackets which protect and describe our editions are unique on the shelves of our existence. They reflect you and me in our individuality. They speak of our journeys. You and I are works of great art. The quiet museums of our worlds invite appreciation. We need to appreciate one another with respectful gazes and the delicate brushstrokes of our creation. I believe in an incredible, very talented eternal artist who calls all of us, in our ways, to mirror his wonder.

When I was much younger, the knowledge of my mortality did not take up a big part of my consciousness. Getting old was something way in my future. It is more present to me now. I easily recall the times in my life when I already faced my mortality, even as a young man. There have been three times in my life when I thought my end was near. These incidents were split second realizations when I realized I could not count for sure on any tomorrow. The first happened when I was a young missionary priest studying language and culture at a school in Cochabamba, Bolivia. I found myself cringing in the confines of an awning covered doorway of a shuttered marketplace with other petrified people. We had found ourselves in the middle of domestic warfare, a local battle between two Bolivian military brigades. A tank had stopped at the intersection near where we hid. I can still hear the rumble of its engine and the clanking sound of its treads, as it came near. I remember the turret of that monster machine turned towards our location. The small group I was with huddled together in the doorway of some shop. A soldier pointed a machine gun from the turret of the tank. He was sweeping the area. I will never know if he was aiming or terrorizing, but I thought I was about to die. Then I heard the growl of that vehicle's engine as it moved away. The second time I thought my time was up was when I was a police officer. A large truck crashed into my police cruiser head-on. I heard some first-responder share, "He's not going to make it." Obviously, this prediction was wrong, but I did not know that at the time. The third occasion when the reality of my demise hit me squarely in the face was in a doctor's office. I heard him advise me that I had cancer. Thoughts of mortality have not been strangers to me. Today, though, the idea is much more familiar. Age will do that, and maybe a pearl of growing wisdom.

Chapter Six: Twists and Turns

Going back to my yesterdays, I thoroughly enjoyed many activities, even as a kid. I was a boy who loved being outdoors. I enjoyed playing baseball in the parks near where I grew up. I was never an outstanding player. I was always good enough to be on various teams. I also loved to swim. I was good at this. A neighbor who was also a swim coach at a local Catholic school had taught me when I was just a little boy. In my whole time learning how to swim with him, I never saw him go into the water. I loved playing at war in the woods and fields that somehow grew in the middle of a city neighborhood. We carried our toy rifles and spent hours digging our foxholes. Some of the kids that shared in these make-believe battles would in not many years be in the absolute horror of Viet Nam. The rear-view mirror is a nice way to see things. Sometimes it is very sad too.

I loved to roller skate. I loved careening down the sidewalks and steep driveways of my neighborhood. When I was a seventh grader, the excitement of indoor roller skating became a reality for me and my other grammar school classmates from Holy Trinity school. Most of us found ourselves crashing into each other and falling hard onto the wooden floors of the Skating Palace, located in the North end of Hartford. Music and laughter filled this place. Skaters of all different skill levels and ages sped around the floor. We could flirt with the girls and then go outside and smoke our hidden Camel or Winston cigarettes. Those were good times for me, especially when I wasn't home.

There are few activities I have enjoyed more than the many hours of reading that have added to my understanding of this journey I have had the honor to travel. Many years ago, when I was a young graduate student, I promised myself that I would read at least one book per week that had nothing to do with Theology or Psychology. These were my areas of concentration, and I needed a mental break from Paul Tillich and Carl Jung. I do not know if I could call reading a hobby. I understand that few things in my life have brought me the meaning and satisfaction of delving into a book.

The reality of our lives is that we all have memorable moments. We all have what we can quickly call unforgettable times. The contradiction of our moments, living in each of our memories, is also the reminder and knowledge that not all unfading junctures are joyous. The irony of our lives is that actually light is also often shadowed by darkness and gray. I am a perpetual learner. I am a seeker. Opening a book to discover the joys and sadness of another's life and times has been one of my most meaningful pastimes. I have heard reading described by some as an escape from reality. I have never agreed with those feelings or that assessment. For me, the experience of glancing into another person's mind and heart has been an experience of discovery. I have had the pleasure of walking through some yellowed northern wood, investigating the diverging roads, and the whispers of meaning calling out to a poet named Robert Frost. I have driven through the depths of America's journey as I imagined sitting next to the author John Steinbeck, with his faithful poodle "Charley," riding in his 1960 GMC pickup truck. I have sat quietly with one of my spiritual guides, the Trappist monk, Thomas Merton. I knew that my own experience was like his. We both knew the darkness of doubt as we prayed for guidance in the silence of beautifully stained-glass windowed sanctuaries. He shared his restless spirit with me as he climbed his seven story mountains of life. I know that I learned from his journey. My prayer is that perhaps you might remember from mine.

Most of us have heard the story about the wolf in sheep's clothing. I remember this as a story of caution. It reminds me that appearances can be so deceptive. I know this is a truth I share. I am a young man in an older man's body. With a less cynical view, we all know things are not always as they seem. I smile as I sit here trying to type these words. My thoughts come so quickly. I am frustrated at my lousy typing skills. I realize that I am like that wolf in that sheep's clothes. I will vehemently deny any other assertion. My self-image is not the old guy with graying hair and added wrinkles who greets me every morning in the mirror as I take various medications.

I feel young, maybe in my thirties! I hope in some way that I also think young. I very much know that I am open to many realities that are new to me. I am not a grinch or a grouch. I have a deep appreciation of history, my own, and my worlds, but I do not keep my focus on my yesterdays. I am not a "back in my day" kind of guy. I live in today's moments. I look forward to what tomorrow might bring. I know, though, that I am now an old man. That aged guy in my mirror is me, as hard as it is for me to admit and believe. Time has passed by so quickly. Those sands in that hourglass keep on dropping down. That is why my moments have become so very precious to me. I wouldn't say I like wasting time on toxic people or toxic experiences. I write with the genuine knowledge that I have far fewer tomorrows than all of those many yesterdays from my other times.

I have been aware of my health for most of my life. Fitness seems even more important to me today. My attempts at staying fit these days are helped immensely by my wife, who helps me keep watch on what I eat, and in my case especially, how much I gobble down in each setting. She knows a great deal about food and its preparation. Her mother was the stereotypical Jewish mother who passed on beautiful recipes and an outstanding talent for baking to my wife. My mother was an excellent cook, but I inherited none of her skills for this. I can boil water, but my brother, Bill, is the cook. My basic knowledge of culinary skills is limited pretty much to boiling water and turning on my Keurig coffee machine. I try to stay emotionally healthy by accepting myself and others as we are, without judgment. I know very well that I am far from a perfect human being. This self-awareness is not always easy. I know that my personally hurt feelings can make this effort almost impossible. I also know that I am not alone in my failings. I keep reminding myself that no one is perfect, including me! I am trying hard at this game stage to be less condemning and more forgiving. This attempt begins with my dysfunctions. Acceptance is not always easy for me. I am very aware that judgment is a toxic brew. Poison kills. I am trying very hard to avoid such mixtures and the people who might try to serve them to me.

Forgiveness plays a significant role in my emotional balance. It is the other side of the coin of love. I also know that my health depends on my spiritual well-being. This reality motivates my deep abiding search for meaning. Our world is a place that appears so often in its history to be without understanding. I have a deep ongoing search for meaning in a sometimes-meaningless world. I do believe there is an ultimate reality that we humans refer to as God. I also think the man named Jesus is my way, my truth, and ultimately my life. I believe that God is love. I think this reality is eternal because I am convinced that love is eternal. I believe that everything I know about Him is from the life of a poor Jewish carpenter. He has taught me that God is love and we who live in love live in God and that this very same God lives in us. My faith is the cornerstone of my spiritual well-being. If I am candid with myself, perhaps my commitment to my wholeness, my physical, emotional, and spiritual health, is reflected in my wish to write these words. I have a feeling there may be some truth in that possibility.

I have had a unique thoroughfare. The irregularities of my own varied experiences fill my path. It certainly was not yellow-bricked. I couldn't call it straight and narrow either. A very apt description of my road would be very winding and not often well-traveled. Have you ever hesitated before you ventured into a lonely nighttime area? Sometimes that was me. Some areas were very dark. Light-filled other places so well that I could hardly see in the bright glare. Others were different sections stretched out before me. They were further along sometimes, dark and forbidding. Some had jagged rocks jutting up from the ground, hiding nearby deep ruts. Sometimes, I fell into some deep groove and got hurt.

Then there were those time-to-time instances when sages pointed to safety and offered me direction. They held weathered signposts, which, time had proven accurate and safe. I listened to some of those who were wise beyond my years. They seemed to know the way. I still got lost. Occasionally the road seemed surreal. I could hear the playful echoes of smiles surrounding the schoolyards I came across. The happy music of innocence filled the playgrounds.

Further along, sometimes, there were bright gardens of beautiful hues. I was blessed then and still am to know some who had planted their lives there. Their kindness and goodness nurtured those very grounds. Even their memories still do. There were also the meadows, more grown in the shadows, and unkempt, mostly filled with weeds. These were the places where the conjurers roamed. They looked normal. They had homes and jobs, and many even went to churches of various faiths. They were not as they seemed. They had many faces and were not as they appeared. They were not caring and lived very selfishly. They were not concerned about God or trying to do His will. They were vain even in their words of humility. Sometimes, along the way, there were inviting waters to cool in and refresh from the day's thirst. This pool is where the sirens swam. They were beautiful and called to me of tenderness and touch and experiences I had never known. They promised safety to the weary traveler. The waves near those shores were passionate and wild. They pounded and crashed against the forbidding landscape. I could hear promises of loveliness coming from far off that shore. Invitations sang to me from way beyond my shore. I should have known better. Thousands of years ago, the writer Homer told of beautiful creatures who lured sailors off course to their destruction by the loveliness of their song. I was like those travelers from so many centuries ago, swimming out toward seductive melody. I almost drowned.

Even as I write, I wonder now about what I should share. I have learned from so many people, some of whom did not even realize they would be my teachers in vital lessons. I try to decide who I should tell you about and what were some of those lessons that graced my life. I am a grateful learner. I look out at the clouds floating by in the blue sky of my world. They are like my memories living for so long in the firmament of my soul. I have stood stunned over broken lives and broken promises. I wonder at the loving sacrifice and dedication I have seen in certain families and unique individuals. I have cried, too, sharing the hopes and fears of a terminally ill thirteen-year-old boy. I was with him when a doctor told him that his life would shortly end. I have walked with drug addicts on the blackened streets of their existence. I have known the reality of being helpless.

I remember a young woman draped over a toilet bowl, convulsing her life away. Maybe she heard her baby screaming from a nearby room. I will never know if she listened to the approaching sirens of assistance. I have wondered about the splinters of broken dreams and the sadness of souls. I saw the grief of my soul too. I decided, once upon a time, to leave the ministry of the Catholic priesthood. I would trade in my cross for the badge of a police officer. I saw the worst and the best in people. I know what terror means in my own heart and experience. I came within seconds of life and death. I have listened to the screams of a man burning to death and been unable to save him from this horror. I have felt the life ebb from a beautiful young girl, dying too young as I tried to administer first aid and saw her begin to disappear through my tears. I have known the aloneness of the celibate life and the loneliness at times of marriage. I have asked deep questions of myself all my life. I have come up with some answers. This wisdom is ultimately my purpose. Perhaps I will help you discover responses to your questions as I have finally answered some of my own. I have tried to be a protector and white knight. I am very aware that I have not always succeeded. Sometimes, my armor has been very tarnished. I think that you and I have asked many of the same questions. Perhaps, sharing my thoughts and feelings along my way will help you find answers along with yours. My days are now taking on the shadows of night. I see the shadows lengthening. I still want to be a light-bearer.

The vocation of love is my best answer to the reality of my definition of me. I need to be for someone other than me. Everything I have pondered in my studies of psychology and theology, even my understanding of history and literature, all tell me that a meaningful life must be loving life. I realize very well that I have lived very selfish moments. These have been times all about just myself. Life has not been good for me during those times. I know, finally, that I must decide every day to say "yes" to those in my life who so beautifully say "yes" to me. I have to affirm those who do not accept me as well. This experience is the challenging part.

Acceptance is where my faith comes in. I believe that my countenance is a reflection of God's presence in my world. I only have a small space where I walk. He loves without condition, accepts without constraint, and forgives without need. That is what I have tried. I have mostly failed in these efforts, although I still try. I know that this is what my creator calls me to do. I have not always been a perfect husband or a perfect father. I have found that family is the best place for me to be a positive influence and a good example. It is also that exceptional place where my God calls me to say "yes" to others, without condition, so I can also say "yes" to myself. For me, this is the essence of what love is all about. I have had a unique life journey as a priest, teacher, therapist, police officer, politician, entrepreneur, and businessman. These all have a very real and deep common denominator. Success to me is defined by how much I have helped others. I have gotten tremendous personal satisfaction when I have done this well. Alienation has crossed my brow when I have not. This effort requires, again, the decision to go above and beyond my feelings. There have been times when feelings have stopped me in my tracks. I know that the resolution towards goodness is a real commitment to others. It is a decision that every day requires my mind, heart, and soul. It is my daily undertaking toward my fulfillment. Awareness, too, is why I write.

Chapter Seven: A Good Life

A dear friend of mine died the other night. His name was Michael Wiseman, but everyone called him Mike. He had been in the hospital for a few days and passed away just three days before his 99th birthday. He had fallen and telephoned his daughter to let her know that he was on the floor and had no idea what had happened. He had a brand-new Apple cell phone, had ended the call, and was no longer answering. His daughter phoned my wife in a panic. She could not get him to answer his cell phone as she repeatedly tried to call. We drove very quickly to his address. We lived much closer than her, only eight miles door to door, from our home in Simsbury to his in West Hartford. Mike had recently been diagnosed with some form of cancer. An examining doctor would make no predictions of his time. He was a veteran who had lived ninety-eight years, and offering treatments or surgeries made no sense. It was not a good sign that tumors had started to show themselves on his back, and they were starting to bleed. A visiting nurse had been with him that day to clean these areas and change his bandages.

He had written a doctor's appointment on the calendar of his kitchen. I remember turning into his driveway and being struck by the darkness of the night. As we walked up the stairs to the front door, the little white house seemed blanketed in darkness. We saw our friend slumped in his favorite lounge chair when we entered the front door. Donna thought he was dead. My police training kicked in. I checked the ABCs of first responders, his airway, breathing, and circulation. Mike was alive. He opened his eyes, smiled at me, and shook his head back and forth in confusion. There was no memory of what had happened except that a fall had occurred somehow. He looked ashen, and blood covered his shirt. His daughter had called 911, and the first responders came into the home and began their evaluation. As they took our friend from his home, each one of us knew that he would never be returning there. I think he knew too.

It was 1941, and this seventeen-year-old boy lied to enlist in the Army. Japan had attacked Pearl Harbor, and Hitler threatened all of Europe after invading Poland and France. This kid begged his mother to tell the Army recruiting officer he was 18, and she agreed. They were a Jewish family from the North end of Hartford, and Hitler had undoubtedly made his fierce hatred of the Jewish people plain. I do not know if this played a part in Mike's decision to enter the Army. His life's most significant and proudest time was his time in the U.S. Army and his service to his country. He was a character. His presence in my life added so much meaning and understanding and lots and lots of smiles. One of my favorite photos of him is standing next to a troop truck on the beach in Anzio, Italy. He is holding an M-1 rifle slung over his shoulder. He is a short, skinny kid wearing a uniform that looks a little big for him. He is also wearing a big shit-eating grin. The photo is black and white.

There are no clouds in the surrounding sky in the background. It was a gray day. A hot piece of shrapnel from an exploding German shell wounded Mike not long after some other young soldier had been struck. I imagine Mike and the other young men fearing for their lives. They must have been petrified as a horrible and deadly German artillery barrage rained down on the American force from fortifications hidden in the hills surrounding their beachhead. Mike would eventually get the revered Purple Heart medal in recognition of his wounds that day. He told me many stories about his Army days and the days afterward. He never told me the specifics of that day in Anzio, only to say, "It was terrible" and that the "heroes are still there." One time he pointed to his chest with his thumb, moving his head slowly back and forth. He quietly shared, "It was awful," summing up his experience of that day. I can only imagine some of his horrible memories.

As we both enjoyed our ice cream sundaes at a favorite local restaurant, he once shared with me that every day after he was wounded was a new day of living for him. This insight has had a significant impact on my view of reality. He lived a long life of 98 years. For him, every day was a new beginning. That smile, that grin, and that conviction defined his life. Mike filled every day with fond recollections of a family that loved him dearly and friends that cared greatly about him filled his days. His time was also brimming with proud memories of his service and happy thoughts of good times with his family. He had no time for regrets. Mike shared my love for motorcycles and told me many stories from the several cross-country motorcycle trips he had taken with his wife. He had known a home filled with the sounds of three great kids, some dogs, a rabbit, and even a monkey! During his final days in the hospital, he told me, "I've lived a good life." He certainly had. His stories of those many seasons are a gift that lives cherished in my memory. Those recollections have added to my understanding of my life as well. I hope my sharing does the same for you.

There is a significant difference between existing and living. I think we all realize this on some level. I am not sure, though, that we all understand how powerful this difference is. My friend understood this intuitively. I think that many of us, myself included at times, get so wrapped up in the reality of daily life that the experience becomes nothing more than breathing, eating, and sleeping. Joy and love can be the exceptions in our history, not the rule. One of the last things Mike said to me was, "Hey, Chick. It's all been good." He did not just exist. He lived.

I have no idea how much time I have in front of me. As I am sure you also know, none of us knows the time or the hour. I have a profound sense that my thoughts and feelings, my sharing of my hopes and dreams, may be a gift for you as you walk your way into many of your tomorrows. I am a spirit-filled man who deeply knows there is a season for every purpose under heaven. Our lives all speak to the variety of life's different cycles. The *Book of Ecclesiastes* affirms that our days have other moments of meaning. I have not always understood these various seasons. I have always known that somehow my God was in those moments.

Sometimes, I have walked very clearly in the light of His day. Other times, darkness has filled my walk, lessened only by my hope that my faith had meaning. One of my cherished stories from the Old Testament is the story of Moses speaking to God on the Mountain in the *Book of Exodus*. This prophet hears a voice coming from the depths of fire. When he asks the burning bush, who should he say is speaking from those flames, God does not answer with an identity. He tells Moses to go back and tell his enslaved brothers and sisters that I AM has sent them, and He is salvation. All those wandering people needed to know is that God is. He exists. My faith tells me this is true. I am a spiritual guy who believes in the same unknown Being who called the Israelites to their meaning and redemption. I can't describe Him. He is way beyond my understanding. My words are so inept at even trying to represent Him. But I do believe, and my conviction is firm. I also think that one day this Word did become flesh. His name would be Jesus. His historical life would teach me about Who spoke in the burning bush and through all of the Old Testament prophets. I also believe that He still speaks through prophets, even today. God is love, and we who live in love live in God and God in us. Ultimately, understanding this fact and its implications have been where my search for meaning has always been. I have not always loved well. I have always known that God calls me to do just that.

I share these word words with a lot of mixed feelings. I have had a life filled with so much and devoid of so much. I do not share this awareness with some sense of deep regret. I mean it only as a statement of fact. I have beautiful memories of being very loved by my mother and father and fondly recall the smell of the Italian sausage grinders my father brought from the South End of Hartford. He would often surprise us with a Saturday afternoon feast, where we all laughed together like most happy families might. I also look back at a childhood filled with dread as I listen to the echoes of anger shouting within its walls. I look back at adolescence as more concerned with meeting expectations held by others instead of trying to discover and live my own. I know now that there was a lot of well-intentioned manipulation instead of decisions of choice and freedom. Many years later, I found who I was when I finally had enough courage and pain to step out into my own life. I left the priesthood on a discovery of whom I might become. This search would be an exploration that would last a lifetime. It continues even as I write these words at this very moment.

As you can see by now, I am sure "once upon a time" has no idyllic meaning for me as I try to share my way with you. I am at that stage of my life where I have way more memories of former times and people and so many fewer promises to keep or hopes to dream. Finally, now I begin.

Once upon a time, I was a young priest. I reflect on the early days of my new calling as I directed the many programs of a large counseling center in Ipswich, Mass. I wanted to enlighten the world with my deep psychological and soul awakening insights into what my faith meant to me. I look back now and sadly smile at that foolish young guy who was so arrogant in his ignorance. I had such ready answers to the soul wrenching questions of many who came to me for my help. Somehow, I was gaining a reputation in the greater Boston area as someone who understood people and their problems. I was teaching at a Catholic high school, sharing my insights about Jesus during this time. I loved every minute of this time, and hopefully, one or two kids learned something that might have meant something to them. I was also teaching at the Deer Island State prison, off the coast of Boston, and at the Charles Street Jail, in the city of Boston, all about the words of the poet John Dunne and the deep emotional suffering from the suicidal Sylvia Plath.

I had begun numerous youth groups, hoping to keep young people out of trouble. Jagger was one of those kids. He was a runaway and slept most evenings in the subway halls near Brighton Avenue. I often met Jag for coffee in a little shop at Kenmore Square. I had originally met him as he had panhandled near a busy subway entrance. His biggest issue was not the many pills he took daily to chase his demons. We spent hours discussing his relationship with his father, who demanded too much and expected too little of a son. He was a kid who only wanted to please. The last time I saw Jagger was as I got onto the train at North Station, heading back to my home in Ipswich. He was a slim kid and his ragged old blue Navy pea coat, missing some of its buttons, seemed to hide him in the crowd of people on the platform of rush-hour passengers. I told him that one of us had better learn to sew, what with the fast approaching winter. I saw him wave and disappear onto the stairway. I never saw him again.

I have always felt an enormous need to heal. I understand now, after many, many years, that this is a deep-seated reflection of my desire for wholeness. I received my Master's degree in Pastoral Theology from the Washington Theological Coalition in Washington, D.C. I also had the opportunity for graduate studies at the Medical College of Virginia in Richmond and later at the Beckley Appalachian Regional Hospital in West Virginia. I was graced with excellent teachers and fantastic opportunities. I was fortunate and blessed to share my pastoral counseling skills with adolescent kids dealing with the reality of cancer in Richmond and the impoverished survivors of a dam collapse known as the Buffalo Creek Mine Disaster in West Virginia. The irony of this period of my life is that every counselor I studied with or who shared group therapy sessions with me told me that my choice of a celibate life was not a good decision for me. They advised me that I was a young man with excellent clinical skills. Some even wanted to hire me away from the Church to head up various teams on their counseling staff. Each told me I would never be happy as a celibate priest. They realized I had a tremendous need to be needed. I respectfully disagreed with their assessments. In my heart, I knew they were right. I chose not to listen. I was afraid to.

Chapter Eight: Other Times

I grew up in a typical middle-class neighborhood. If you ever imagined a nice street with well cared for houses and lovely trees in each yard, that would describe where I grew up. Our block had no picket fences, but it was still a great place to grow up. Our home was in what was known as the South End of Hartford. This area was where many Irish and Italian families settled at the beginning of the twentieth century. Numerous well kept two and three-family homes lined the streets of this area. We lived on Broadview Terrace, and the houses were mostly Cape Cod style homes. Ours was too. It was not a big home, but we had a good size front yard with an old tree that my brother and I used to climb regularly.

We also had a large backyard, big enough for our Labrador Retriever, Blackie, to run for some distance, hooked onto a long chain attached to the clothesline, which stretched the yard's length. We had a tree fort back there too. We had a gang of kids in the neighborhood, and this was our secret place, a rickety structure that we had somehow nailed into a plywood shack 20 feet above the ground. We hid our cigarettes there. This hideaway was where we also stored old Playboy magazines. These treasures were usually wet and weather-worn because we hid them in leaky old milk crates. There were some larger homes in our neighborhood too. Living in such prominent places, I always thought these people were more affluent than us. Looking back, they probably were. I remember one house, especially, because a boy who had polio lived there. An iron lung encased his body. He looked at his world from a large, round mirror. This reflection showed all that was happening in the front yard of his home. I do not know of anyone who ever went to visit him. I only saw him two or three times when I passed by the house on my nighttime paper route. I do know that

I saw a smile reflected in that mirror. Everybody had nice yards in our neighborhood, with small lawns proudly mowed and edged. My young neighbor from across the street would never walk on any of them.

I was eight years old when we moved to this new neighborhood. I have a recollection somewhere deep in the back of my mind that we had moved to this neighborhood because my father thought this area was supposedly healthier for my asthmatic brother, Billy. Maybe my recall is all wrong. Until third grade, we lived in a crowded neighborhood with no yards, many old apartments, and dilapidated garages. My father owned a three-family on this street. There were also numerous brick tenement houses and a lot of foot traffic between those places and the local package store, where some locals brown-bagged their drink of the day. This neighborhood was where we spent the first eight years of our lives.

Perhaps my father was right, and our new home would be a healthier place for us. I have to wonder whether our recent, frightening experience with a child predator, who had approached my brother and me with a friendly pup, might also have played a part in our move. My brother and I had told our father about this strange man. He approached us in front of our house. We were leaving to walk up the street to our school. When we came home, we saw an ambulance in front of our house, a lot of police cars, and a bloodied man lying on the ground with his hands handcuffed behind him. My father was standing over him, nursing a broken thumb. I think this might have been the moment of truth for my father as he decided that we would move from that neighborhood. My brother's health was the reason he gave to us. By the time Billy was sixteen, the dirty blue smoke from the Royal Typewriter factory on New Park Avenue had no apparent effect on him, and my brother had no cough.

I look back on another time just after we had moved into our new neighborhood. A pack of neighborhood kids, eight of them, began picking on my brother. It soon became evident that they would not let us pass along the sidewalk toward our house. I was not a bully but had my own experiences in schoolyard fights, even as a young schoolboy. I knew that we had to fight. One of the bigger kids was Pete, who would become a dear friend. I gave him a bloody nose that day, and he ran home in tears. His mother came out onto the front porch and screamed after us, "Get home, you bloody Micks!" I didn't even know what a "mick" was, but we indeed headed for home that day. My mother told us that "mick" was a bad word that some people used when referring to Irish people. Those boys in that neighborhood group would eventually welcome us to the area. We would all become close friends. We shared each other's yards, tree houses and classrooms, baseball bats, and gloves for the next eight years. There was a big field out behind my house where locals grew vegetables during the Second World War. It was called a Victory garden, and we all spent many happy days wandering through its paths and overgrown fields. We also used to fish in the Hog River, which ran through that area, never catching any fish. Many years later, I would learn that this river was so polluted that even city workers did not like getting near it.

There were no trout or perch to add to a successful Saturday afternoon, but we had good times and made many good memories in the place we called "The Vic." We also shared our Irish, Italian, and Portuguese foods and families. It was a good time for all of us until later when it wasn't. Many of these guys, Dave, Tommy, Rocco, Mike, Jimmy, Al, Charlie, and my brother Bill, would later answer Uncle Sam's call during the Viet Nam war. Uncle Sam did not reach out to me. I thought Jesus needed me. He called me when I was in eighth grade. I decided to answer. That response would wound me too. Our various answers to God and country forever determined what our lives would be for many years to come. Many of us thought then that we had all the answers. We were so very foolish.

When I was ten years old, I woke up at 5 a.m. most mornings because I sold newspapers, standing on the corner of Hillside and New Britain Avenues. I hawked the *Hartford Courant* to the early morning workers, most of whom were heading to factories, and some, like my mother on her early bus, to the telephone company. Other mothers went to secretarial jobs in the many insurance companies for which Hartford was famous. Sometimes, I would see my father drive up in his State Police car, getting honey-glazed donuts and onion rolls, across the street in the Brookside Bakery after a long and busy midnight shift cruising the highways of Connecticut. I loved my time as a paperboy. Looking back, it gave me a great deal of confidence to stand on my own two feet. It also gave me a steady income to buy cigarettes and commemorative stamps, which I avidly collected from all over the world, especially from Vatican City.

This interest in the Vatican was another subtle hint of experiences to come. I also saved money for Saturday morning movies at the *Rivoli*, where some kids claimed to shoot skinny gray rats with big black eyes with their slingshots. I remember once or twice getting free candy from the old drunk who worked behind the concession stand. His name was Stanley, and he lived in a run-down apartment up the stairs from the filthy men's room. He looked like every picture of death I had ever seen, with his thin, mottled pale face and uncut, unkempt greasy hair. He always had on an old black trench coat. Stains from various dried-up liquids, some of which were probably alcohol, covered much of this old coat. He had few teeth, and the ones you could see when he seldom smiled, were yellow with brown, probably coffee stain. His hands were black from the ground in dirt, and he was not a nice person. I never bought popcorn from Stanley. Tommy Shea did once, and so did his fat sister Mary. They both got very sick and had terrible diarrhea for three days. I did not suffer the same malady.

I grew up in a very Irish Catholic family. I had two obligations in this world: to please my parents and God. These were the bricks of my youthful existence, and guilt was the mortar that held this world together. Looking back, I grew up trying to please my mother and father to such an extent that I never looked for my own hopes and dreams until many years later. I now understand that God calls us to love one another as much as we love ourselves, not more. I am not called to live someone's dreams. I am meant to discover my own, and those who love me will appreciate the person I am.

Do not let anyone else's wishes for you become more important than your own

---

Sometimes, these will be the same, but when they are not, please choose yourself first. Otherwise, you may get into the terrible habit of putting other people's needs ahead of your own. I have fought this battle my whole life. I implore you to decide not ever to walk this road. It might be a more leisurely journey for some time, but it will never be a better one. Find what you love to do, and do it. This affection may change over the years, but please always do what you love, for yourself. I am not an expert in these matters. Often, I tried to please others first.

One time, I caught sight of the sunshine's brightness reflected through one of the stained-glass windows in the church, and I saw Jesus standing in the glass. He had a tan, a lovely white robe, and a bunch of kids sitting at his feet. I remember seeing many other religious figures peering down from their windows as I walked from the back of that place of worship, between all the flower vases, to the sanctuary where I would be ordained. It was a beautiful April day, and I thought about how chilled I felt and how warm it was outside, with almost May temperatures and just a slight breeze blowing. I remember being very nervous and looking out the door on the side of the altar, seeing so many people coming up the flowered walk. Seminarians had worked weeding the surrounding gardens for many days and preparing the roses. My mother and father came up the sidewalk. Nothing would ever be better for either of them than this moment as they led the parade of our family up the long path. No moment before in their lives and no time later would ever be compared to this time. Their son would prostrate himself flat on a polished floor, before their Irish God, in the company of their Irish family, in the presence of an old Irish bishop, and that same son would stand up, a Catholic priest.

I can still see the stained-glass windows I had seen hundreds of times before as I had prayed in this church at the La Salette Shrine in Ipswich, Mass. I kneel in silence, begging God to help me with the lonely sadness that wrapped my life. He never did. The ordination vestments that I would soon wear covered dark old tables. I was struck by how costly they were. I was self-conscious putting them on. I was a poor kid out of Hartford's South, and suddenly I felt out of place here, even after twelve long years of preparing for this day. I should have run for the massive doors, and run, and run some more. I did not.

I was with two other twenty-seven-year-old men as I consecrated my life to the priesthood. I was nauseous and hoped I wouldn't throw up as we all answered in unison the Latin words "ad sum" and "here I am." Here I am, Lord. Here I am, Venerable bishop. Here I am, everybody in this massive church, all you family and friends, and pretty girls I'll never touch. Here I am, Jesus, and Mary and Joseph, with your Holy Spirit. Here I am with your smiling saints, watching from the sun-reflected windowed views. Here I am, Uncle Ed; you too are a priest, in all your priestly robes, and Auntie Nip, have one for me. Here I am, about to become a priest, and all I could think of was how cold this very chilled, polished floor was. We lay on the floor during the ordination ceremony. I looked over to my left. I saw the soon-to-be priest, my classmate, Father Luke, positioned there on the tiles of the sanctuary, with his Jesus beard and white robes. I whispered, "This floor is cold!" He gave me a dirty look.

The ordination ceremony is finalized with the questioning by the Bishop of the man to be ordained. My journey to those questions had begun many hesitant years before, or maybe just a day ago. I kept telling myself that perhaps I could get out of this before it went too far. I knew, though, that too far was already happening. It had already gone far in all those years of study and preparation. Too far was already over! Mr. Unsmiling Bishop had already pronounced those sacred Latin words of ordination: "*Tu es sacerdotum aeternum.*" "You are a priest forever," The Bishop rasped, "Are you ready?" I answered, "*Ad Sum,*" yes, and thought, *Are you kidding?* "Are you able?" I heard him rasp in his barely audible brogue, muttering into the microphone for all this party to hear. I answered, "*ad sum*" again, "yes," and thought, *I am able.* If I am anything, I can please serve and wait for the crowd to lift me in celebration. O Yes, Bishop, I am able. And the old man put his gnarled hands upon my head and told me I was now a priest, "According to the Order of Melchisedek," whomever the hell that was. My ordination ceremony was the end of a journey for me. It was also a beginning. There had been many chapters before this moment. There would be many more afterward.

Chapter Nine: Tattoos and Other Memories

Washington DC is one of my favorite cities. I enjoy the uniqueness of each of this city's neighborhoods. Some areas filled with fabulous little restaurants gave my inexperienced dining experience new tastes in sandwich wraps and coffees. Many of these had outdoor seating, so eating was always fun while people gazed simultaneously. There were other areas where whole blocks were sections filled with college kids trying to figure out what was happening the following Friday night. These busy streets reminded me a lot of Boston with its numerous colleges, except in D.C., the names were Georgetown, Howard, Catholic U, and a wide variety of others. Fourteenth Street has long been the place for bars, tattoo parlors, and a couple of strip clubs that had been there for years. Night in this section of town was like a rite of passage for many serious-minded students like myself. It was that place for many of my first hangovers, the first bar fights, my first dancing naked ladies, and maybe even my first love. Of course, there were not a lot of future priests walking these streets back then. I did not go there often, but I have spent some pretty rollicking times in some of those places. They were unique classrooms for me that were an amazing and sometimes hilarious part of my graduate school education.

An old, nondescript building was one such location. A dimly lit sign that showed a tattoo invited me to a dark cellar location. I should have been very wary when I saw the steel bars on the windows and glimpsed the hidden hulk in the corner, becoming the tattoo artist as I walked into the area. I remember having had a lot of beers and a lot of wishing for some ink art on my arm. The creator of the blue flowers, which he forever memorialized on my arm for all of my life, was a short bear of a person covered in wild colors. When I told him how much money I had, much less than I needed, he pointed a 45-caliber pistol at me and told me to "Get the fuck out." I quickly left that parlor with my unfinished tattoo and memories of too many beers. Washington is also home to marvelous monuments dedicated to our history and heroes, which are well-traveled by millions of people each year. I also spent a great deal of my time visiting many of them.

Despite what some of these memories might imply, I did go to Washington to study. This city became the center of my education world for three years. I loved walking the paths of Catholic University and being instructed by world famous theologians, who were not only questioning traditional theological assumptions in their published works but also the very structure of the organizational Church. I would study for three years within its hallowed ivy walls and within the corridors of the Washington Theological Coalition, which was also a part of my educational world. Every day I walked with other young men on our various pathways to the Priesthood. Some would get ordained. Many of us would also leave.

Once upon another time, during those three years of graduate school, I met a homeless man who taught me more than many professors and assigned me term papers and bibliographies. His name was "Slim," and even after all these years, I still vividly remember the many wonderful times we had drinking our hot coffee on some not so hot mornings. I have such fond memories of those conversations. There was a narrow bridge near Monroe Street, and I often met this homeless man as I walked to my classes at the University. I would bring him hot coffee with "lots of sugar, Chick," as he always reminded me, from a hole-in-the-wall place on 14th Street, down the road a bit from the Monroe Street firehouse. I would sometimes bring sugared donuts, especially crullers, made fresh that day. Slim would bring me his stories from a place in his memory often clouded in cheap booze, especially wine. I do not think he knew how important his friendship was to me, but I looked forward to sharing coffee and stories with him as often as possible. He wore the same brown and dirty old army trench coat daily and told me about his days in the First World War. Sometimes, I would bring him new socks or underwear and share stories of my days, which were nowhere near as fascinating as his. He told me about the Argonne Forest in France and the brutal fighting he witnessed there. He was only a teenager and told me how he had seen "too many" soldiers die. Then he would become very silent and drink his coffee.

Slim's story was a booze soaked summary of many painful moments. Before going to war, he wanted to set type on a printing press. Being wounded in those hellish woods of France changed that forever. He returned from fighting on the rusted troop ship that carried him to his fate. He looked for a fiancé who had promised a future to him. When he arrived back in New York City, he found neither. He did not see her, and with that loss, he did not find his future either. All those tomorrows would be a time gliding along on the alcoholic rivers of cheap wine and sad memories. He was the very definition of sadness for me. So many wounds and hurts and heartaches, never to be healed. I guess that's why bringing that over-sugared coffee meant so much to me. It was a huge deal to him. It meant so very much. He became special because I made him very special. He made me feel exceptional too. This affirmation taught me. It was another lesson I learned in D.C., not in books, but in the tattered gratitude of an almost friendless man. Slim knew he meant a great deal to me. I knew I meant a great deal to him—two poor men who had discovered some wealth. We acknowledged one another and accepted ourselves as we were in that recognition. I was getting a hint of what God's love was like, not in a theology book, but in the smile of a caring derelict whose gaze accepted me without any conditions. I would also discover new experiences in D.C. not found in any of my books.

I fell in love for the first time in my life in D.C. Her name was Maria, and she was from Mexico. She was taking classes at Catholic University, where I met her. We both loved discovering the many insights psychology brought us, and eventually, we would become transparent in the thoughts and feelings we came to share with one another. I had been schooled for many years that it was possible to live a healthy, sexually abstinent life. Looking back, the men who taught me those lifestyle lessons were celibate. Perhaps, none had a "close" relationship with anyone but Jesus. I do not know, and I certainly do not want to judge. I do know, though, shocked to my core, that some of them, seven I knew, would later be identified as monsters.

For more than a few years, especially as I began my summer vacation, I spoke with my father about the possibility of leaving the seminary. He always said my feelings would change once I was ordained, but I had to stay. The Viet Nam war was raging too, and I wanted to go into the service. I had even written to the local draft board to see if I could have my draft Status of 4D (Clergy-Deferred from Service) changed to 1-A (Available for Service). I was advised this was impossible unless I was no longer a member of the deferred class.

Leaving the seminary had been on my mind since my first high school summer. My friendship with this wonderful Mexican girl brought that possibility to the forefront of who I was. Eventually, I would depart from clerical life. My father and mother would disown me for the disgrace I had caused them with this decision. The organizational Church would also disavow my choice, and I would reject its celibate statute. My God would still whisper, "Come follow..." "Come follow...," and I would finally have the courage to do just that, but it would be my way. These consequences would become the inevitable results of this unique D.C. experience of closeness that blessed my life for the first time.

Maria loved being with me. We hardly understood each other's language, yet for two years, we happily affirmed, laughed crazily at each other's jokes, and listened intently to each other's dreams. She was the first woman I had ever met who was attracted to me, physically, emotionally, and spiritually. I smile as I write these words. I was very attracted to her. She had a sense of freedom about her, which was new to my experience. She was a beautiful girl with long black hair, which she sometimes wore in long plaited braids. She had dark eyes, which she sometimes hid behind oversized round sunglasses. She had a smile that made me melt when she shared it with me. I loved her sense of humor. This young lady was among the most joy-filled people I have ever known. She made no secret of her affection. This admission was a constant temptation to my vows, which I somehow managed to keep. She was the only person I have ever known who used the word "beautiful" when referring to this guy, her fellow traveler. I treasure that memory to this very moment.

We were both just kids, twenty-two years old, and so sure of many answers as we faced our futures. How foolish we were. I realize now that I was. There were also many doubts, at least for me. Although I didn't even know it then, I was still an adolescent in so many ways. I had never dated. My adulthood was significantly delayed because of my time as a Catholic seminary student in the all-male world. Here I was, so concerned about breaking my vows that I did not realize I was crushing my soul. That insight was not a part of my consciousness.

Maria went home at the beginning of my third year of Pastoral Theology graduate studies. Her father was a lawyer in a small town in Mexico, and her mother had died three years before of cancer. She had a large family, and Maria wanted to help fill the gap which her mother's passing had left. Sometime later, this wonderful friend would finish her studies in Mexico City and eventually become a psychologist. She wrote to me once, just before I was getting ordained. She wished me much happiness in my life and invited me to her home if I ever had the chance to go. I did not, and I never heard from her again. I have sometimes thought of her in fond reminiscence of those times. There were frequent Friday nights, sharing cold beers in frosted mugs and hanging out at a dingy college hangout on 14th Street. Sometimes, on Saturday, we went to the National Zoo, where we imitated the monkeys as they imitated us. I think of the many days we rode my old motorcycle back and forth to Catholic U. I think of all the times an elderly priest sat on the front porch of my residence on Monroe Street and waved with a big smile as we drove by. I sometimes think that he might have envied us.

I studied Pastoral Theology for three years in Washington. I finished my exams and defended my thesis for my master's degree, "Use of Self in Crisis." Some failed these exams on the first attempt and were not allowed to defend their thesis. I remember going before a board of six stern-looking professors who questioned me for what seemed an eternity. I passed this inquisition, and my insights into clinical psychology and pastoral theology were somehow accepted. I felt tremendous relief. Many had not been so fortunate. They would either stay in DC or travel to campuses throughout the country. They would continue their studies in preparation to retake those exams. Some extended their time in the seminary. Others settled for a resume without an advanced degree.

I headed north to the Our Lady of LaSalette Shrine in Ipswich, Mass., where I would begin and direct a counseling center. I was a year away from being ordained, and I spent some time working with teenagers, many of whom were runaways and involved in drugs. I formed a youth group called Reach Out, dedicated to "helping good kids stay good kids." I taught English at Deer Island State Prison and the Charles Street Jail in Boston. My evenings were filled with counseling and teaching, and I felt tremendous satisfaction in helping people understand themselves and others. My self-awareness was cloudy during this time, and doubt filled my nights with the sadness that would eventually cause me to leave the Priesthood. The journey to that departure would take me seven more years of confusion and soul-searching.

Six years later, while studying in Bolivia, I would have some idea of what some of my friend Slim's fears must have been those years ago in the trenches of the First World War. I crouched in a doorway, listening to the rumble of tanks on the war-torn cobbled streets of a military district in Bolivia. I remember cowering in fear with fellow students attending a language school in Cochabamba as I watched a turret turn towards us. The gunner never fired, but I remember the terror I felt that he might. This recollection is one I will forever have.

I would also learn about the dread of living under a murderous military regime in Argentina. I observed the small black cars of the government security forces following college students as they strolled along the park paths of Cordoba. These operatives also followed business people, journalists, artists, clergy, and anyone suspected of opposing the right-wing dictatorship. During the ten years between 1974 and 1983, this Argentine government murdered over 9000 civilians, and thousands more simply vanished. They would become known as "Los Desaparecidos," the ones who have disappeared. Their mothers and grandmothers have come together in a group, Las Madres de Plaza de Mayo, that seeks justice and information to this day.

Anyone not in favor of the military-led dictatorship was potentially in danger. I knew about this before I went to Argentina. On some level, I had made peace with the possibility that I would not be returning to the United States. A member of my missionary community had been detained there for some time along with five seminarians. They endured physical beatings and death threats, although, thank God, they were eventually released. Many others were not. I had no doubt then or now that I might have ended up on some government list if I had stayed in Argentina. Life can change in a moment, forever, for better or worse. Our realities depend on how we each react to those times, some totally out of our control. My experiences in South America taught me this insight in a way that I had never known before. This lesson would be one that I never forgot.

Chapter Ten: Not My Circus

L ife is sometimes a rollercoaster, with its rickety ups and downs, terrifying drops, and maddening ascents. I know my life has been like that sometimes, filled with the fear of the unknown coming around the next corner. Some of my most enjoyable childhood memories have been near those giant wooden scare monsters that always seemed central to the fun parts of my earliest days. I smile at those thoughts, recalling my special moments at amusement parks. Perhaps the most famous of those places for me and my brother and maybe one of the oldest locations where people of all ages go to experience a good time is Coney Island in the Bronx, New York. I proudly proclaim that I enjoyed its many sights and smells, tastes and sounds when I was just a little boy of eight years old. So did my brother and father. I remember that day.

It was like a kaleidoscope of thoughts and feelings. There was a food place called Nathans. It was a small building near a corner in the park, and a long line of hungry people, primarily kids, waited for their delicious serving of hotdogs, curly fries, and crunchy pickles. It had a big green sign with white letters, proclaiming that they had the best hot dogs in the world. I know they tasted that way to me. The smell of the sauerkraut covering the deli-style mustard and the barbecue sauce that drenched the hot dogs seemed to be part of the air everyone was breathing. Most of the ground was asphalt and concrete, and it seemed like a million pairs of feet were clamoring along their way between all the different rides and attractions. There was always a massive crowd of people walking all over the place, and everyone was in a rush. There was a tall, one-hundred-foot wooden slide whose stairs to the top seemed an endless climb for my short seven-year-old legs. We got ready for our turn to fly down this gigantic slide. The highly waxed finish made the ride an experience of speed and excitement. An old man who looked barely sober handed out rough burlap sacks to sit on. It was wonderful. These rides were all enclosed in a building called Steeplechase Park. Every inch had people rushing back and forth, with the whole place filled with laughter mixed with the sound of a giant organ playing loud music, which I could hear plainly above the din. Kids were running around with red candied apples and balloons of all colors. Everyone carried a smile too. My brother and I did too.

Many years later, I volunteered at the Danvers State Mental Hospital, where there wasn't much laughter. This facility, built in the 19th century and once known as the State Lunatic Hospital at Danvers, was initially meant to provide humane residential treatment and care for five hundred mentally ill patients. Over the years, decreased funding and staffing made this impossible. I met a patient named Susan O'Neil, who called this dismal place home for several months. It was just a few miles north of another seaside amusement park, Revere Beach, in Massachusetts, an area filled with wild rides and crowds who shared laughter and smile-filled memories. I doubt Susan ever experienced much of that same delight. I encountered some wonderful people at this institution. Many staff cared, and some patients found healing or a sense of peace. Some did not.

I remember that locale of overcrowding and urine-smelling hallways, where over two thousand unfortunate patients with various mental illnesses made their home. Susan lived in the area called the J3 Ward. I remember that place as a locked unit for those deemed harmful to themselves or others. That area is where I first met Susan. She lives in my memory as a beautiful, sad girl who looked like one of my favorite folk singers, Judy Collins. J3 had a television mounted on metal brackets, high up on the dingy green walls so patients couldn't reach it. There were rows of black and white chairs. They were plastic, so if a patient threw one, it would not cause severe damage to staff or residents. This area was known as the community room, where patients spent the entire day unless white clothed attendants restrained them in their rooms for negative behaviors. The place was always dreary, and thinking back about the times I spent there, I do not remember seeing many nurses, aides, or orderlies smile. I am sure these employees were all caring people, but budget cuts and overcrowding did not create a positive work environment. I guess happiness died eventually for most who walked these corridors and were later somehow reborn in the safety net of family, alcohol, hallucination, or prayer. Susan escaped the dreariness of the place in the silence of her tears. She often wept and sat alone, looking blankly out the wire-meshed windows, with her legs folded up on her plastic chair. This place was no church, but I do know I prayed with Susan here, sometimes in quiet words of petition. Maybe this young lady heard her God's whispers in that place's silence. I hope so.

I doubt Susan ever had many good times. She probably never even tasted the sweetness of that blue cotton candy that filled the faces of young people running on an old boardwalk not five miles away. Her hands were perhaps never sticky with the gooey feel of yellow taffy or even held warm three-ringed pretzels dripped with salt and yellow mustard. From our conversations, we did not share similar childhoods. Mine was filled with early memories of laughter and, later, maybe more tears as I grew toward adolescence. Her memory bank was misted in hurt and held mostly darkness and thoughts that were grief-filled. I had caring people in my life. Sometimes she had her mom and then just me.

I met her mother in the hallway once. She was very Irish and very much an alcoholic. Once she had been pretty too, a long time ago. She was also grateful that I regularly visited her daughter. She did not. Susan had no idea where her father was, or for that matter, who he was. He had disappeared from her life many years ago and from her memory. I remember looking at her arms. They were scarred with the deep, ugly wounds of razor blade cuts, and grotesque gouges that hinted at horrible times. Susan seldom spoke with me but always hugged me whenever I walked into the hallways of J3. She had been an A student once and an outstanding athlete only a few years before her hospitalization. Her mother had told me that Sue had been a swimmer and a swift runner. I saw a colored photograph she often carried with her, holding it like a precious flower as she walked the hallways. The photo was bent, but this now sad young lady stood proud and lovely with her track team of other happy and jubilant teenage girls. She told me that two local colleges had awarded her partial track scholarships. She had never accepted them.

The Community Room was the place on the ward where patients gathered. Most sat around old round tables and played cards or checkers. Susan always sat alone, watching the tv bolted high up on the wall. It was on a shelf, anchored out of anyone's reach. Others preferred their own company and sat alone, sometimes staring blankly around the area. As I visited this unit, I wondered if some were so medicated that interest and enthusiasm had long since departed their lives. I think that, at times, medications were prescribed for patient treatment and control. I do not know for sure. Often, Susan sat alone in that community room. Sometimes she would sing an old rhyme from her hometown, not to anyone, but quietly to herself. I still remember it: "Lynn Lynn, City of sin. Once you get out, you never get in."

I asked her once to write to me about one of her talents. I knew she had a beautiful voice and excellent athletic ability. I remember her gaze as she looked at the piece of blank paper on the brown card table. She took the crayon from me because pens and pencils were not allowed to her. She drew a large black circle, smiled sadly at me, and wept. As the months passed, the day of my ordination to the Priesthood quickly approached, and my visits to Danvers State lessened. Susan was released and I would never see her again. Later, she got very involved in drugs and alcohol, hanging around the dingy bars of Lynn and Revere Beach.

I looked for her many times after I had taught my English classes to some prisoners in the Charles Street Jail in Boston. This fun place long ago disappeared from the Boston horizon, but after my classes, I would drive along Route 1A, heading north towards Ipswich, by the beaches along what is known as the North Shore. I always hoped to catch a glimpse of her. I never did. I have a feeling that she did not stop weeping. I remember her telling me, "I just want to be somebody, Chick." Ultimately, that need is what we want in our lives too. The tragedy of her life was that her tears could never cleanse her soul. Neither could my words or my care. A state cop called me one night and told me she had died alone, from an overdose of heroin, in an emergency room at St. Elizabeth's Hospital. Again, I experienced the tragedy of a wonderful human being who died because she could not see her beauty or believe in her loveliness. I believe that the affirmation of my possibility demands that I also affirm you. The saddest people in my life have been those who could not make this sometimes-whispered utterance to themselves. Life can be so fucked up sometimes, like riding a terrifying rollercoaster.

Three little monkey statues sit quietly on a bookcase in my home. It is not a big bookcase, just four shelves tall, and the monkeys live on the second shelf from the bottom. They are quiet. They are not big into fun times but sit more reflective and almost somber. They are serene. They speak volumes in their silence. They speak to me, sometimes loudly, even in their stillness. I wish I could hear no evil, like that little guy sitting there on the left side of this trio with his hands so tightly covering his ears, blocking the ugliness of lies and cruel words. I wish I could say I have never seen evil, like the monkey in the middle of this trio, with his hand so fully covering his eyes. I also wish I could speak no evil, like that third little monkey, with his mouth firmly covered by his hands. Many years ago, I learned about these three wise little monkeys. They were born in the Shinto religion of Japan, where they became humble reminders of good living. They have also become my tutors: Kikazaru, who hears no evil; Mizaru, who sees no evil; and Iwazaru, who speaks no evil.

I sincerely believe that my God whispers to all of us in the quiet of our lives. I know from my own experience that the existence of my loving God has been through encounters with loving people, who have reached out to me, acknowledged me, and sometimes forgiven me. I also believe that the cries of the infant in Bethlehem and His anguish as a convicted rabble rouser, criminal, dying tortuous on the cross of Calvary affirm that I have value in the eyes of my God. He loves without condition and ultimately forgives me for my selfishness and meanness. I believe He lives and, most importantly, we are Him for one another. I also know that Faith is a leap beyond the darkness of terror into grace and meaning. God has said "Yes" to me, affirming who I am. Somehow, I respond with my "Yes" to Him. I am convinced of the words of John's Gospel, that "God is love and that we who live in love live in God, and God in us" (1 John 4:16). These words would eventually take me away from the pulpit and into a police car, hearing not the echo of hymns but the piercing wail of sirens. I would no longer listen to the quiet confession of sins from a penitent fearing God and covered in a mist of guilt in a darkened confessional. Instead, I would sometimes hear the panicked cries of fear and anger echoing from an assault victim covered in blood and breathing in gulps of hurt and pain.

God has been the central reality of my life, as I ran to Him or sometimes crawled. I have also rushed away from Him, walling myself in as I separated myself from others and ultimately from myself. I have lived in the darkness of doubt and guilt. There have also been times when I stood tall in the joy of love and forgiveness. This experience has been central to my search for meaning. This quest continues, even as it began many years ago.

I grew up in a very Irish Catholic family. My God ruled in fear by a lot of rules. My heritage and religion cultivated my youth with a deep awareness of my imperfections. The Sisters who schooled us called them sins, and the parish priests required weekly Confession. My faith was not one of relationship but of obligations, proclaimed quite clearly every Sunday by a sometimes very judgmental and unsmiling pastor. The message I remember most clearly from the religious instruction of the good Sisters of Mercy was not about the joy of God's presence in my life but rather the absolute dread of losing it. Most of these women were good, kind people who taught what they had been taught, a doctrine more concerned with sin than the sinner.

I am sure they did their best to proclaim the Good News, and so did most of the priests. My memory is that my religion back then was based more on fear, not freedom, more on shame, and not forgiveness. I also know I grew up in a time when this view was much a part of the Irish culture. Years later, as a graduate student in Theology, I would learn that many of those early lessons from older times were superstition. I remember a scripture instructor telling our class of future priests that we would all lose our childhood faith due to our studies. He then added that hopefully, we would find it again as we came to a deeper understanding of scripture and its demands on our lives. He was right. I did lose my faith, at least those guilt-driven beliefs from my youth. I thank God that I eventually found it.

Our ability to remember our histories significantly impacts our ability to define who we are. I find it fascinating that my earliest memories have filtered out the loud shouting and dysfunction which would live in later recollections of my adolescence. I remember the long walks to a local park with my mother and brother when Billy and I were five years old. I remember running ahead on a busy street and my mother hollering to me to wait for them. I remember listening to an outdoor polka band at a city park on Sunday afternoons. My mother and father sat on an old picnic table and clapped to the joyful music as my brother and I ran around between the seesaws and the swings. I remember bus rides to downtown Hartford, where we would eventually enjoy ice cream treats in the crowded basement luncheonette at Brown Thompson. Hartford natives called it BT's. It was my mother's favorite department store and her favorite place for lunch. Sometimes, we went for hot dogs at Sage Allen. My mother enjoyed shopping there as well. Most of all, I think she enjoyed her boys sharing smiles with her, and having good times.

My father was not a shopping kind of guy. He loved circuses and railroad trains. When we were little boys, my brother and I shared those times with him. I remember going to carnivals and feeding hay to the massive elephants. Huge chains held these gigantic animals to thick iron pegs pounded into the ground. I still have photos of my brother and me, with a couple of neighborhood kids who joined us, as we stand next to a faded red wagon cage that held some old lion or tiger. I remember riding in my father's state police car and going for hot meatball or sausage grinders on the Berlin Turnpike, or ice cream at Tina's Diner, now long gone. We had front-row seats for Friday night wrestling matches held at the National Guard Armory in Hartford. We watched in awe as we saw giants with names like Yukon Eric and Killer Kowalski throw each other around the ring. I still remember my father's cruiser call sign of KCH-788. I love these memories of times spent with my mother, father, and brother. They are the bedrock of my belief that life is basically good, even when sometimes it is not. They remind me that not everything is negative, even with occasionally painful recollections. Some of my negative reminiscences are not as clear as those good times from my earliest childhood. Perhaps, that is a good thing.

I have an imperfect memory. I smile as I recall my high-school seminary English teacher, Fr. Bill Hart, sharing that one of my favorite authors, Mark Twain, thought his memory was that place where, as a boy, he could recall everything, whether it happened or not. I am not quite at that place. My thoughts about my yesterdays are all true, but I have found that the passage of time somehow softens the painful remembrances. I know that I have hurt others profoundly, and others have also hurt me, some very deeply. Somehow, with my aging, there is now a different context. I have more sympathy now for others and for myself. There is more forgiveness and a greater willingness to understand. I find this especially true when I think of my parents and their influence on me. I believe they did their best. I am trying to do that as well.

I am a religious guy with an abiding sense that a Reality beyond myself calls me to find the deeper purpose that He constantly whispers into my life. I believe deep in the heart of my very being that my God has great expectations for me and that He calls me to live up to them. I do not believe in the God of my youth, who was the Eternal Scorekeeper of right and wrong. I am not keeping score either, but I know I insult my Creator when I choose to be less than I know I can be. That is my definition of sinfulness in my own life and yours. I do not believe that He is a Bayer aspirin in the sky. I cannot take Him three times daily and think He will cure all my ills. I now know my prayer is my asking stance before God in humility, to please let me understand and follow His Will, even when I do not fully know what it is. I do not believe that God wants me to depend on Him but that He wants me to say yes to His presence and His Light, even in the darkest of my nights. I do not have an answer to all the evil I have seen in my life and world. In my inept understanding, I know it has something to do with what we have called "original" sin.

Once upon another time, I spent much of my life trying to convince people to believe in God. Now, I walk in silence sometimes, just in awe that He believes in me, very personally and lovingly. My response to this understanding is my calling, my vocation. My God believes in all I have ever been, all I am, and all I will ever be. He asks that I believe in Him as well. My response is what my faith is all about. My prayer is that you never lose faith in yourself. That would be an insult to a loving God.

Chapter Eleven: Yes, I Can

I believe that "Yes, I Can" is, without a doubt, the most crucial sentence I can speak, sometimes, if only in a whisper. I went to South America thinking "Yes, I can" was a real possibility to deal with the aloneness and isolation I felt as a celibate priest. Maybe I could bury myself in my missionary work. I would be so tired or concerned about others that somehow the lonely reality of celibacy would lessen in the hard work of my commitment to the poor. South America was my last-ditch effort to somehow stay in the priesthood. I was so miserable and confused in my ministry in the States. I loved what I was doing but hated the loneliness of my life. South America did not become any cure for this pervasive sadness that celibacy had become for me. Finally, I realized that I had to face myself honestly. The Catholic ministry may have called me, but a celibate life did not. That existence was too painful for me. I look back to when I returned to the States from Argentina. I was traveling to my dreams. I found nothing of the sort.

I enjoy poetry, writing it, reading it, and mainly reflecting upon the profound messages I find in the words of the many poets whose words I treasure. One of my favorite poets is Robert Frost, whose "Death of the Hired Man" holds special meaning for me. A farmworker named Silas is dying and needs to go home, which for him is the farm he had once worked on for many years. Silas is from a wealthy family, but that isn't where he goes to die. The farmer, Warren, and his wife, Mary, are not relatives. They are not pleased to see him, the man who had left them without help many years previous. Warren is very critical of Silas, this former employee, who had walked away from his necessary and needed chores. His wife has hurt his feelings. Her former employee had betrayed her, but she welcomed him back. The hired man named Silas had nowhere else to go. The farm was the only choice for him. He had no place to go other than that old farm. He was finally home. He also found forgiveness from the angered farmer and kindness from his once-disappointed wife. I found no such welcome when I returned from South America.

I loved everything that I did as a priest. I loved the preaching and the teaching, the counseling. I loved being needed by so many. My contradiction was I had no specific, special one who could share in this pride. I hated being home at the rectory and pretending I was a happy guy, with the friendly banter of my fellow priests, watching a Celtics game, or discussing some future parish activity. I had taken a leave of absence from my ministry the previous year. At that time, ultimately, I could no longer bear the dishonesty of my life. I had prayed to God to please give me strength. I would spend hours walking through the woods of the seminary property in Ipswich, Mass., praying from the depths of my soul for the power to stay. In the distant future, my prayer would be for the strength to leave. I almost left the priesthood at that time to marry an extraordinary girl who had come into my life. I might have spent the rest of my life with her. This decision never happened. I was not ready yet, or brave enough.

My father traveled to the parking lot of a Howard Johnson restaurant on Rt. 128, North of Boston, begged me not to "ruin your life." We spent a long time talking. This meeting was maybe the first time I had ever spoken with my father about myself, my soul, my hopes and fears, and my dreams. It was also the first time my father told me he loved me. Some months later, I would write in my journal a very poorly composed letter to my father that I never sent. Lots of regrets filled the sentences.

"It would have been so much easier, wouldn't it, Dad, to tell me a long time ago that I might have meant something to you. Everything I did seemed so wrong. I escaped to lonely streets from a lonely house. I remember where no welcome ever called...where I might be of any import. You never knew the tear dripped heart within this man, your son. Finally, now I know. It might have been nice to hear...those years were so long ago. If only you could

have heard the songs sadly sung in those times of gray, what I was feeling and had to say...and you with your perfect black and white way.... me so breathing such disarray...It would have meant so much a long time ago.... that you cared...why did you have to wait until finally today...."

I spent the following years just trying to survive. I had taken a vow of poverty, and every penny I earned went to my religious community. I had no personal savings. I might have made thousands of dollars as a psychotherapist, teacher, and public speaker in another life. Still, I was a member of a religious congregation with a vow of poverty. The Superior had to permit significant spending, which was a genuine part of my life for many years. My religious community supplied my car, my clothes, and even the room in which I lived. Each community member contributed to the well-being of all. The Poverty vow and the vows of Obedience and Celibacy are the keystones of "Religious life" within the Catholic Church. To live these vows in a community with other men and women who shared the same vocation was considered a "calling." I had done so since taking those vows seven years prior. When I eventually left the priesthood, I no longer had that community. I had no money or family that spoke to me. I had no advisor to turn to, or for that matter, no relatives. I was on my own. This was a blessing and a curse.

Chapter Twelve: Crisis Time

Leaving South America was also my exit from the Catholic priesthood. I had told my church community and superiors of my decision and had written to my parents. My life as a missionary priest might have been in danger. That was a possibility but not a reality. There was a severe threat from a military dictatorship that did not tolerate dissent, and I certainly disagreed with the governing generals. They had already arrested many students, teachers, and clergy. The real threat I feared was the threat to my soul and integrity. I could not continue choosing to live in my priestly world, where violating my vows would become a reality, not just a daily temptation. Ultimately, how we feel about our lives is always a matter of choice. Even as messed up as I was, emotionally and spiritually in those days, I realized that I finally had to be honest with myself.

I remember flying from Cordoba in Argentina and landing at Logan Airport in Boston. When I arrived, I walked outside the terminal and found a pay phone. These twentieth-century communication devices do not even exist today. I had pocket change, but not enough for a long-distance call from Boston to Hartford. I had to make a collect call to my parents in Hartford. I was nervous as I heard the operator ask my father if he would pay the charges for this conversation. He agreed to answer my call. There was a long silence on the line, and then my father told me never to come home. I was in shock. I could hear my mother in the background. She was crying. I heard her keep saying to my father or herself that I had disgraced the whole family. She wondered how they could ever face anyone again. I had shamed them to that degree. My parents never wanted to see me again. My father told me I was dead to them. I was not welcome in their home or wanted in their lives. I heard my mother tell my father to stop talking with me and end the call. There was a long silence, and then the phone went dead. My father hung up.

I remember standing still next to that pay phone. I looked around at all those travelers heading home to their loved ones. I cried. I had eleven dollars to my name and not much more than the clothes on my back. I had no home and no place to go. I feel deep sadness as I write these words, even these many years later. Those feelings still wash into my memory as I step back into that time. My parents abandoned me. I was alone. I was in shock. I walked around the terminal for a while. I did not have enough money for a bus or cab anywhere. I did have enough coins to call a family in Danvers, Mass. who, several years before, had welcomed me into their lives.

His name was John Devarenne. He was a staunch, rosary bead-carrying Catholic who regularly brought his family to my Sunday Masses. He didn't like some of my liberal theology, but he loved me. He drove a delivery truck, working for a local potato chip company. His wife's name was Ruth. She had been a grammar school teacher until she left that profession to raise their five kids, Linda, Susan, Patty, Laurie, and John. Ruth was an incredible mother, nurturing, understanding, and forgiving to each of her very individual children. She considered me one of them and loved me immensely. I spoke to John and explained what had happened to me. I think he was probably shocked that I was back in the states. I am sure he was surprised that I had left the priesthood. I am also confident that he probably disagreed with my decision. He advised me, though, that he and his wife were on their way to get me. I was part of their family, and they were coming to bring me home.

I lived there for several weeks. I slept on a couch in the basement of their small home. The warmth of love from these two beautiful people surrounded me. Their kids were now forever my brother and sisters. Many years later, I would have the immense personal honor of speaking at the funerals of these two so-loving people. They blessed my life with their own. They were the kindest people

I have ever met. For me, they were, and still are, the ultimate example of loving without condition.

I missed the Hartford area. I grew up there, and it was familiar to me. I eventually moved back to continue my journey into the future. I had known an Italian family many years before and contacted them about my situation. This household welcomed me into their home in Manchester, CT. They provided a bedroom for me, and many beautiful meals shared around a small kitchen table with people who cared for one another deeply. I had no direction at that time, and yet I finally had a place to go, a destination. I met this family many years ago when I had been visiting their parish in a small Connecticut city and saying Mass on weekends there. They had lost a son in a tragic car accident, and I had been there for them. I still smile at the smell of tomato sauce that Anthony would spend hours making or the insistence of his wife, Marie, that I bundle up as I went outside to clear snow from my borrowed car. I remember those times too, when we shared tears, sitting on the small front porch of their Cape Cod house, he with his nightly cigar and she with her worn flower-colored housecoat. All of us are still grieving our losses in our ways. I was grateful for their time and their tears. Without their presence in my life, I am not sure what my future might have been. They reflected an acceptance of me that I had not experienced for a very long time. I was so grateful. I still am to this very day.

I have come to believe that not one of us has had a perfect history. We are also very imperfect. This fact has been a major lesson in my life. I, too, am far from perfect. This knowledge is where my faith comes in. I believe that I am somehow a creation of God. I am unique even in all of my imperfections. That is OK. I spent my whole life trying to save people as a priest, later as a police officer, teacher, therapist, and even as a businessman. Ultimately my life has been my effort to save myself somehow too. I listen very closely to my God. I hear him, especially in the silence. I was sure about who my God was when I was a priest. His name was Jesus, and he was my savior. I still hold firm to this faith. I left the priesthood for

1000 reasons. Not being able to marry was the major one. Celibacy was destroying my soul. I could not have imagined living a whole life without the unique love of one specific person and one particular relationship. I tried to do this as a priest. I could not, at least not honestly. I know that the essence of my faith requires being for other people. It also demands that I am committed uniquely to one person alone.

Somehow, my experience after I left the priesthood enhanced this definition for me. I no longer lived on a pedestal but walked next to someone on our journey. Much of my faith as a young boy was superstitious and not grounded in genuine study. Take God three times a day, and all would be well. The study of theology destroyed my early faith, and ultimately as I sit here at this stage of my journey, that faith is whispering yes to a reality way beyond my understanding or comprehension. I sincerely believe that Jesus is the way, truth, and light for me, and I say this after walking in the darkness for many years. My faith tells me that God is love and that we who live in love live in God and God in him. This experience of relationships is the essence of my belief.

A paradox of my life is that my spirituality is more profound now than at any other time. When there are more years behind than in front, that may seem the obvious route of thought. Even as a police officer, I tried to live the expression "To Protect and Serve." These words have more religious significance than many of the phrases I read in the prayer books of my more Catholic days. I grapple with my decision not to go to Church. I still miss the rituals of the services I once led. I once had experienced the smell of smoke rising incense as almost a prayer. I miss that too. It reminded me constantly of my prayers reaching somehow to my God. I sometimes miss the sense of community that I also experienced. I do not forget the loneliness.

Yet, I found a much deeper sense of togetherness within the reality of law enforcement and even later within the confines of a corporate office building. I guess my feelings of estrangement from the organized Church had been growing for a long time, even before I was ordained. I never liked wearing the black suit of a Catholic cleric. The Church's stance on birth control, celibacy, the reality of the thousands of abused and damaged kids destroyed by pedophiles, and my view of a clerical class has brought me to another place on my spiritual journey. Here's a contradiction for you. After years of going to daily Mass, I stopped going to Church. This choice is not necessarily a better place for me than those who still attend, like many of my relatives and friends. It is my place. I find God in the experiences and people of my life and in the graced silence of my walk. My church experience is now pretty limited to weddings and funerals, and I say this without judgment of myself or others.

Chapter Thirteen: The Thin Blue Line

I became a member of the Farmington Police Department in 1980. Farmington is a suburb of Hartford. When I became a cop, the town had about fourteen thousand residents. The police department was one of the highest paid in the state. That was a big motivator for me to apply there. Many police officers throughout the state also considered it to be among the best trained, which was very appealing to me. It was a small department of fewer than 60 men and women, highly professional and with a deep sense of pride among its officers. I was proud to count myself among them. I still am proud.

Back then, I was still always a young man in the shadows of my ancient history. The police department was located in the old Town Hall basement and boasted a dispatch area, administrative wing, three jail cells, and our roll call room. A magnificent new building replaced this many years after I left law enforcement. Our roll calls were very much a part of my everyday life. Men and women who had accumulated many years in law enforcement comprised my day shift squad. We were a diverse group. I reflect on those days and miss the camaraderie I shared with all the other cops who sat around that table. Our K-9 officer was a female officer whose courage and care marked her career. There was a Corporal whose professionalism reminded everyone that working with pride was sometimes way more than just responding to a call. There was a Vietnam vet whose wounds from that war merited him unique respect from each of us.

Most of us had some college, and some had college degrees and had been in other professions before becoming cops. Then there was me, the former priest with a ninety-credit master's degree in Pastoral Theology with advanced training in crisis intervention and counseling. What a picture of differences. We were men and women. We were black and white, men and women. Some were veterans of Vietnam and others had never served the country. We were all united, though, is a genuine dedication to being good cops and good people. We were quite the crew and still are. Most of us were not loving the early morning in the squad room, listening to the sergeant's report on stolen cars, missing persons, recent crimes, and suspicious circumstances, and wanted people to know. Happily, one of the rookies brought in coffee, and the world was all good again. Our morning roll call was pretty standard that day. It was late April. The morning sky was deep blue and cloudless, and the yellow flowers in the gardens near the police department, daffodils, I think, were starting to bloom. The six o'clock morning news had forecast the day to be mild and sunny. I never thought someone would die in my arms that day. I remember the blood.

The officer in charge was a sergeant who was a grizzled old-time cop with many years in law enforcement. He was the epitome of discipline, and when he ran a roll call, everyone knew very well that there was no bullshit allowed. I loved this guy. He had over thirty years in law enforcement and left no doubt that he was all business. He lived his conviction that being a cop was the finest calling any person could proudly live. There were no exceptions to the discipline he lived and expected from others. He was not only a good cop. He was a good man. I would be honored many years later to give the eulogy at his funeral. It was one of my proudest moments. He usually finished his roll call with the advice to stay safe and keep others safe. This dedication to one another and the community was what being a police officer was all about.

Police officers share a unique, exclusive, private bond that no one who has never worn a badge can understand. Once a police officer wears that badge, a cop joins a brotherhood and sisterhood of a family whose heart beats pride, whose soul lives integrity, and whose very being is filled with the adrenaline that only fear and courage can cause.

No one else knows the feeling of walking into a dark building, searching for a prowler, and not knowing the violence around the next corner. No one can understand what it is like to be in a fight with a non-compliant husband, who wants to continue beating his wife, and now wants to fight you. No one can relate to the experience of walking up to a motor vehicle and watching someone reach for a gun as you un-holster your own. No one else can know the sense of dire necessity, driving with lights and sirens and responding to another officer's call for help. No one can ever know what it's like to be that officer. I know that some have dishonored this calling and their badge. They are the very few among the very many.

When I was on patrol, I always paid particular attention to motorcycle riders, especially younger ones. The roads were sometimes still covered with leftover winter sand, making riding a bike a little more dangerous. I was young once, and I remember the love of speed I experienced as a new motorcycle rider on my first bike, a blue and white Triumph 650. I was pretty foolish at the time. I had been riding a motorcycle since my teenage years, and now I sometimes rode one as a police officer. I remember speeding down Route 84 and marveling that I was getting paid for this exuberance. I would be assigned to the police motorcycle today and was delighted with that. All was well with my world. I kept busy responding to the routine calls for service, but I did not run radar on the motorcycle. Still, when I saw someone going beyond acceptable speeds, I often stopped the vehicle for a conversation and a verbal warning. We only gave written warnings for equipment violations back in my day. My visual speed estimates surely did not fit that category.

I saw the oncoming Harley approaching. It was a beautiful bike, and the rider had prepared for the day with good leather and a black helmet. He was wearing a beautiful pair of motorcycle boots too, and I remember telling him I wanted some like that when I got rich. We were in a 45-mph zone, and he went by me doing around 60. He waved, and as he saw me turning around and activating my emergency lights, he quickly pulled over and took off his helmet and gloves as I approached. He was a young man in his early 20s. He told me he had been riding for four years and, with a smile, asked what I would have done if he hadn't stopped. I answered that he couldn't outrun Motorola, and we both laughed. He admitted to the excessive speed on his new bike, which was more powerful than he was used to. I told him I was giving him a verbal warning, hoping there would not be a next time. We both got back on our bikes and bade each other goodbye. Neither of us could have imagined that a "next time" would soon be impossible.

About five minutes later, the dispatcher sent me to back up another district at a motor vehicle accident with injuries. As I approached, I saw a cruiser was already at the scene. Beyond that cruiser, I saw the mangled Harley. I could see the patch of sand where it had slid. The bike was lying in a puddle of oil and gas. Then I saw a boot, out of place on the shoulder of the road. Then I saw a young man, covered in blood, crumpled, and lying on the side of the road. I ran to him as I heard other sirens screaming in the distance. He was still alive, barely, and paramedics arrived as I was holding him. He died before they could provide any assistance that might have saved his life. Sometimes, I think of him, especially when I see young guys on bikes. I wonder if I could have done anything more to slow him down.

I saw a lot of death as a cop. Some were medical calls, where I got there too late, although still usually ahead of other medical personnel. There were some incidents where we had to bust down doors or finally get them opened with keys provided by property owners. Frantic, out-of-state relatives or caring friends or co-workers, and sometimes nosy neighbors would call the station to ask for a "welfare check" on an individual who had not been seen or heard from in some days. Often the rooms were dark.

Suicide is this country's tenth leading cause of death, and this was, at times, a part of my day. Thankfully, not very often. I remember responding to such a tragedy. I forget who notified the station, but I found the door unlocked when I responded to the residence.

When I entered, the first thing I saw lying beside a brown leather recliner was the .38 pistol on the rug. Seated in the chair was a middle-aged man who had shot himself through the mouth. His teeth, flesh, some of his brain matter, and lots of his blood covered the floor and splattered on the nearby wall. There was a very distinct odor filling the space of what had been someone's home. Death smells, and anyone who has stood by a corpse is familiar with that odor. Sometimes, that odor would stay with me, even as I was driving on patrol many hours later and responding to other calls for help. I had to wait for the Medical Examiner to come to the scene and certify this death. Gruesome sights are horrible, but they never physically affected me. A rookie who also responded to this call rushed outside as he felt like vomiting when he first saw this terrible ending. I advised headquarters that he would be clearing from the area and that I would be staying at the scene. My response to this crisis was one of calm and control. I remained, and that young officer left. That was the proper decision for both of us. Seeing a violent death is never easy. Police officers get used to it. That new cop would too.

I arrested hundreds of people over the years. I also found some missing children and returned them to grateful, anxious parents. I sometimes fought people who resisted arrest or drug addicts and drunks, too intoxicated to know better. I found myself separating couples in violent marital disputes, which always end in an arrest. I also had my share of foot chases, running after teenagers who had stolen items from a local mall or bailed out of a stolen car. I also saved some lives. I was a new patrolman then, and I still remember the six-month-old little girl whose breathing had stopped as her frantic mother had called 911.

I arrived at the house even as the mother was still on the phone. I began CPR, and the baby started to breathe! That deep feeling of the satisfaction of saving a life remains with me today. Two years later, I would respond to a medical call in the same neighborhood, about a mile away. I found the screen door unlocked and rushed into the home. I saw the thirty-year-old young mother who had been frantically calling for help moments before. She was leaning over the toilet bowl in the bathroom at the top of the stairs. She was dead. I do not know the specifics of the autopsy results. I am sure it indicated that she had died of a cocaine overdose. I heard an infant boy crying in a crib nearby, but the white residue I saw was not baby powder. I left that scene very sad. I remember crying as I drove down that street on my way to another call.

Chapter Fourteen: It Is All About Us

My experience of police work is that officers always felt that three groups made up our domain. This community of cops was a unique reality. Our world involved shared shifts. It involved shared roll calls. It involved road jockeys, driving around for hours in police cars that sometimes smelled of leftover cigarettes and sweat. The brotherhood-sisterhood of police officers defines the family of blue. Every day the news speaks of the "Blue Wall." I am a proud member of that remarkable edifice. We saw ourselves as the only people who knew what reality was. It was "us" against the "world." We were the ones who knew the experience of driving with lights on and siren blaring. We were the ones who shared the fact of wearing a thirty-five-pound gun belt as part of our everyday business dress. We were the ones who lost sleep and marriages over the sights and sounds of our daily lives. We were the ones who had been spit on, puked on, and pushed on as a somewhat regular part of our work schedule. We were the ones who could, in the utterance of a sentence, take a person's freedom away in the experience of an arrest. We were the ones who could take life away in a fraction of a second or lose our own. Yes, we had an inside seat, the front row of this circus called life. We were a tired crew, but we knew the reality, which wasn't pretty most of the time. No one else shared this knowledge.

Then there was "Them," made up of the so-called law-abiding citizens. These were the folks who knew nothing about police work or crime until their lives might be affected by both. These were the same ones we, as police officers, had sworn to protect and serve. These people were the people we had been once upon another time. These were the folk whose most considerable excitement during a specific week might have been a strike in the last bowling game or trying a new pizza at the local shop. Some less fortunate had concerns about feeding their kids or where the next unemployment check might be arriving. Problems, rightfully so, were about school boards and tax rates. None of them worried about getting home alive each day and helping others do the same.

The last group who made up my world were the "Assholes." These were the criminals, or as was often the case, sometimes people who had decided to make poor choices, which ended up hurting themselves or others profoundly. Drugs created a 19-year-old drug addict, whose addiction caused him to rob and burglarize. I arrested him as he tried to break into his parent's home, a place that long ago had been closed to him. Gang members were also "assholes." They love to steal cars, and during a midnight shift, I saw some of them running through dark backyards, trying to avoid arrest. Numerous officers responded to my call for backup, and we eventually arrested four young men who did not have a very successful evening. I held a long black flashlight, known as a Mag, in one hand and my nine-millimeter SIG Sauer pistol in the other. I almost shot an off-duty fireman who had come into a blackened area when he heard the sounds of running and voices. He was carrying a gun for his protection. He would be forever grateful to me for not shooting him that evening. I have been forever grateful as well.

"Assholes" were sometimes violent spouses who left their supposed loved ones bruised and bloodied. The black and blue coloration on a tear and blood-stained face always denied a suspect's claims of innocence or protests of outrage. I hated responding to family disputes. They were dangerous and sad. There were so many victims, some very young. These were the kids who shared a parent's tears and fears and forever painful memories. Some of these recollections remained for years.

There was a wide variety of people in our "Asshole" group. They often hurt others and threaten violence. Usually, they blame someone for their rotten lives and poor choices. I once apprehended a burglar right after he had jumped out of a rear window of an occupied residence. He had a pipe in his hand and began to walk toward me. I pointed my weapon at him just as I heard my backup officers running my way. The thief begged me to shoot him. He finally dropped the pipe and dropped to his knees. I still remember his words as I ordered him to the ground. "Nobody would give a shit! I am so tired of this." He was talking about himself. I know he was also probably talking about everyone in his life. He was in his early twenties, and I felt sorry for him. I have always known that building bridges to other people's lives was more important than building walls. As a cop, I sometimes had difficulty separating the criminal from the crime.

We all share similar judgment experiences as we relate to the different people in our worlds. We assess our thoughts, feelings, and even physical contact that we share. The irony of all these opinions is that not one of them is ever wholly accurate. I have often found the non-verbal communication of others to be much more accurate. I do believe actions speak much louder than words. I have also discovered that our perception of others can become the less-than-perfect conviction of how we see people. Sometimes, that perception is false. I remember seeing the mourners at a funeral as I spoke words of comfort from a distant pulpit. Some would show no emotion as they buried a child or loved parent. They felt immense grief but also a cultural need to appear strong. I remember looking into the rear-view mirror of my police car and looking at the impassive, unflinching face of some individual I had taken into custody. As I processed this person, taking photos and fingerprints, I would find out later that they were petrified as they sat in that back seat. I would find a profound sense of remorse and sometimes a profound sense of guilt. Poverty, addiction, and hopelessness can sometimes make people do some pretty horrendous things. Perception, in truth, is not always reality.

Ironically, in dealing with some so-called "good" people, I sometimes found that my view of them had been wrong too. I remember one guy who regularly met me at a McDonald's, where we shared morning coffee. He bragged about his two sons, who were very active in sports at a local school. He often bragged about his wife, a hardworking homemaker working part-time at a local convenience store. I would later arrest this man on assault charges in a violent nighttime confrontation. Responding to a dispatch regarding a neighbor who had heard screams, I found his wife on a front stairway covered in blood and bruised. She told me that he had told her once that no one would ever believe her if she called the police. I did believe her, much to the chagrin of her husband. He cried like a baby as I put him up against his living room wall, searched, and handcuffed him. Perception can be the reality for most of us. The truth is that our observations about one another are seldom as they seem. Police work confirmed this truth. It is also true in life.

I think this knowledge separates individuals who know one another from those who rely on perception alone. Knowing someone is much different than mere observation. I guess the real question is how many people do we know? I once lived stereotyping many other people. I was a priest, a police officer, and a businessman. These various occupations offered me a lot of protection but also kept me distant from myself and others. We only really come to know who we are as we share this knowledge with others. Perception is the reality for many people, but it is not valid. The truth is that we only build bridges when we tear down the walls of judgment. Police officers often are the first to admit that this guy did not seem as bad as he was, or that guy did not seem as good. They might affirm that this cop did not seem to be as racist as he was or that cop did not seem to be so violent. Viewpoints about others can be misleading. In my journey, building bridges takes honesty and constant learning about myself and others. I tried to tear down the walls that separated law enforcement from the greater community in law enforcement. There was no longer "them" and "us." All of us are a community, whether we like it or not. My goal has been to protect and serve this community for much of my life. Sometimes, I was not able to do either. This sentence haunts me.

I could hear the dire seriousness of the call in the dispatcher's voice. Her name was Monique and she was not panicking. She had worked many years behind that desk, filled with computer screens and phones, and did not get excited about anything. She had heard it all during those years of dispatching when she had sent cops to the various situations that their days demanded. I loved when this woman worked the desk.

Calmness prevailed for her. On duty, she got the information right, especially the tiny details that can determine the outcome of a call. Frequently, all a cop needs to hear when responding to an emergency is the tone spoken over the airways. I had learned this over the years, responding to weapons calls, fights, family disputes, and life-or-death medical calls. Occasionally, this voice inflection saved lives.

Off duty, Monique was a riot as well. I laugh as I still look back and see her sipping Budweiser with the best of us. We gathered around an old pickup truck behind the police station, swigging cold beers, after long shifts maybe, or before long days off. We had a lot of good laughs. She often shared on these off-duty occasions when good friends shared good laughs. I have found that laughter is an excellent remedy for sadness. Grief would be coming soon enough.

A few dispatchers were more concerned about sharing coffee and gossip than grabbing the small tidbits of information that added to critical police knowledge. I was glad they were not working.

It had been raining much of that Saturday. It was August, and it was warm. Even as the hot afternoon turned into a cooler night, I could still feel the sweat sliding down my back. The showers were a welcome relief as they cooled the high temperatures of the previous hours. My shift, which had been running from 3 pm until 11 pm, had been quiet until it wasn't. I had been assigned to District 4 that day, and at 7:15 that night, I heard, "District 4, respond to a signal 1B." A Signal 1-B is an accident with injuries requiring a light and siren response. I have responded to many accidents with injuries throughout my career. This would be one more. I reached forward in an automatic motion and flipped on my emergency blue/white lights, my headlight wigwags, and activated my siren. This collision is unique in my life. It haunts me.

That day had crept out of the darkness of the midnight shift. It was gray in the early dawn. I remember jogging near a reservoir and hoping it would not rain as I breathed hard into my second mile. It's crazy remembering that day, but even the three to eleven shift I was on seemed without its usual go-to-hell banter and kidding around. Maybe my memory is just tinged with sadness now. I am not sure. Perhaps hindsight gives me descriptions I did not have back then, but I will never forget what happened that day. It all began at twenty of three in the afternoon. Eight of us were sitting around, drinking terrible coffee that had been bitter in the roll call room for hours.

We were waiting for the Shift Supervisor to assign our duty assignments and districts and share any info he deemed necessary. He would inform us about people to be aware of who was wanted for arrest. He would also share information about stolen cars, their descriptions, and the times the thieves took them. He would also inform us that he would inspect our vehicles on the road. He told us he would ensure that all of our cruiser trunks' emergency equipment was up to snuff. God help the cop who was short of med supplies, flares, or a fire extinguisher. Tomorrow, at another roll call, he would share information about a horrible death I have never forgotten.

Chapter Fifteen: Horror Time

The first thing I saw as I came over the hill in the eastbound lane was the gray rock wall in front of me on the shoulder of the road. I was familiar with that block of stone. It bordered the entrance to a large quarry behind it, and I often parked behind it when running radar on this busy road. My cruiser was hidden from the view of passing vehicles, and I often pulled out from this area and stopped motorists who, unfortunately for them, were speeding by. I am sure it was an outcrop from a granite formation, which had lined this section of the roadway for hundreds of years. I am also sure that flames had never scorched those walls like I saw that day. I saw the line of eight or nine stopped cars blocking my way.

Some, who could steer to the right, drove to the road shoulder to let me pass. Those drivers heard my siren blaring and saw my emergency lights. They also sat transfixed, seeing the burning vehicle in front of them. Other drivers sat in their cars, helpless, unable to move in the line of stopped traffic. Some had gotten out of their vehicles and motioned to me, frantically waving their arms and pointing forward. I saw a trailer truck pulled over onto the shoulder of the road. I saw the driver. He was a fat guy wearing an old blue baseball cap with tattoos all over his forearm. He was leaning out of his cab and pointing up the hill in exaggerated and frantic motions. I vividly remember this trucker. He was shouting and pointing across the road to where the pickup had come to rest. Now, everything he did seems in slow motion, like an enhanced video viewed at a significantly stalled snail's pace. Yet, everything that transpired that day took place so quickly in reality.

Then I saw the old green pickup truck. There were a couple of turned-over lawnmowers in the vehicle's bed. Funny how I remember they were red and still covered with grass shavings. There were also four gas cans. They were tipped over and had rolled against the side of the cargo bed. Gas was leaking from them. I would find out later that the driver had spent the day mowing three lawns in an adjacent city. He was rushing to a fourth job when he lost control on the wet road and slid out of control. The collision demolished the front of the vehicle. It had crashed, head-on, into the stone wall and slid back into the road. A mist of smoke began to cover the truck with a fine layer of gray, almost like dust. The whole scene is like an old sepia photograph indelibly placed in my mental album of former times, a place filled with other memories from other crisis times. I still see the debris all over the road. There was the crumpled silver frame of the right headlight, shattered glass glimmering in the wet roadway, silver grill parts, and oil all over the glistening pavement. The oil, mixed with the water on the road, made a strange rainbow in its puddles. Many years later, long after all this debris had disappeared, I would sometimes still see those parts as I drove through this place.

I would still see the flames too. They were coming from under the hood, now crumpled from the crash. I remember hollering into my portable radio that there was a lot of smoke in my vehicle. The dispatcher responded that emergency equipment was on the way. I knew what was happening right now. The dispatcher I had called at headquarters was pressing a button on her transmitter and calling for various professionals to head my way. Firefighters would be running to their trucks. She was hitting a black button on the gray console before her, and tones would be emitted from various locations throughout the area, blaring from loudspeakers placed on top of school buildings and off of tall wooden poles, that an emergency was taking place. The radios of volunteer firemen echoed those notifications and loudly came alive in cars and on kitchen tables. They shouted directions and information. Emergency vehicles began to roll. First Responders activated lights and sirens, and the rush to save suddenly started. Some volunteers, too, would be heading to another station nearby and getting into their gear. I had been a part of this scenario of law enforcement, fire personnel, and medical responders many times before, coming together like partners in a well-rehearsed dance. I arrived at an emergency scene to save lives. I had been a part of that scenario many times. With these other men and women, I had known the extraordinary experience of saving lives. We had all worked together at accident scenes, fires, crime scenes, and incidents of weather-related damage to properties and people. We all were satisfied knowing that each of us protected and served and had done this well. The next day, I had no such experience.

Age has tempered so many of my memories. Some of them are vivid as if happening just yesterday. Others, not so much. My thoughts are sometimes clouded by the worn shroud of time and experience. Some debris from the trauma and panic of those hours still cover my memory of that day. Smoke was coming out from the right side of the engine and small spits of flame. They were so tiny they almost looked like sparks at first. I still can hear the driver's voice, though. He was screaming that there was a fire in his truck and wailing in a beseeching voice, filled with fear and terror, that I have never forgotten. I have never forgotten his words either.

I ran to the burning wreck, carrying the fire extinguisher from the trunk of my cruiser. I focused on knocking those flames down and extricating the driver. I blanketed the cab inside with the white foam spraying from the extinguisher, hoping to smother the fire. The flame-retardant worked for maybe ten seconds. I was oblivious to the others who had also rushed to this scene, another trucker who would unload his extinguisher, spraying the engine compartment and the cab's passenger side. I remember an off-duty nurse from work in a local hospital. She was standing in the roadway, too, helpless to assist as I tried to pull this man from the flames. They all knew, like me, that this blaze was slowly engulfing him. I grabbed the man under his arms and tried to pull him out. I remember feeling the heat on the skin of my arms before I saw the flames smoldering beneath him, his legs locked into the truck by the crumbled firewall which was crushing them. There was nothing

I could do to dislodge him. I kept trying as I reached into the truck and grabbed under his arms, trying to somehow pull him out. I was helpless and hopeless, too, as I saw the flames begin to burn beneath his legs and creep up his body. His tan work pants were on fire. He began to scream. I remember yelling at the stopped drivers that I needed more extinguishers. They got them and ran to the passenger side, spraying the dry white powder and foam from their devices into the cab. The fire kept coming. I could feel the searing heat. I knew that by now, there were other police officers at the scene, and I could hear the sirens of fire trucks very close now. I do not remember who they were or even what they were doing, but I knew they were there, protecting this scene and feeling just as helpless as me.

I watched the flames engulf this man. I could smell his burning flesh. I stood there probably a foot from the driver's side window. Somehow, I still see bits of his shirt become flicks of ember. I am not sure about the length of that memory. I am sure that I could do nothing. I felt absolute helplessness that I had never felt before. I would experience that again in the not-too-distant future. He screamed for me to shoot him. One of the last things he begged, in a horrible beseeching voice, was, "Officer, you would shoot a deer. Please shoot me!" I read these words now. They do not and cannot convey the horrible anguish of that moment, for him especially, but also for me. I saw the flames consuming him, wrapping him in their blanket of a terrible fire. All I could do was stand by and listen to his screams. I could no longer hold him. The fire and the heat were now a wall between us. The last words I heard him say were, "Shoot me." I cannot imagine the pain he felt in those horrible, agonizing minutes. I know watching him burn to death was awful.

The fire trucks arrived quickly, but it seemed like hours to me. Firefighters doused the inferno that had once been a truck, but it was too late to save. This charred frame was now a tomb. A man had died in minutes. He had burned to death in my arms. I would find out later from one of the firefighters that the flames in the cab had been fed by streaming gas flowing from the overturned cans in the truck's bed. The gasoline had become the continuous flow of accelerant seeping into the cab. This answered why the many attempts to extinguish the fire ended in such frustration and failure. Everyone, including me, had been aiming the extinguishers at the blaze, not the leaking gas cans in the back of the truck. There was no fire back there, and none of us, until firemen arrived, paid attention to that area at all. That scene would come to haunt me. That death and those terrible moments would soon crash into my consciousness. I would be the driver, pinned into another filled vehicle, terrified that I was about to burn to death.

The closeness of dying and the unpredictable reality of sickness and mortality keep me wondering about my life's purpose. Your life is about that query too. I wonder about my yesterdays and their meaning for me and others in my life. The question I seem now to be asking much more is what has my own life been all about? I am more comfortable with answers to this search now that I am an old man.

The pandemic days and weeks, and now years, seemed to be a constant reminder to me, and I imagine to all of us that the reality of death is a regular caller. Those times begged me to be more reflective. Perhaps, it is just my age as an older man. I have added many years to my life's calendar, and my questions seem to ask so much more. I know now that my answers are seldom as absolute as they once were. My life was once filled with black and white conclusions. Now, many gray areas have filled in so many blanks where once simple stereotypes dwelled.

Maybe I have always been one who reflects, trying to find meaning in the unseen or not understood. We all have early memories. As a little boy of maybe five, I remember sitting on the front stairs of a neighbor's house, on South Whitney Street, in Hartford. I was listening to what probably was a record player or radio, but I thought that I heard angels singing. I really did. I am smiling as I read this and wonder what you might think about this recollection. I won't laugh at any of your reflections if I ever come to know them. Throughout my years and studies, especially of psychology, I have had the opportunity for extensive counseling and group therapy. There is much to be said about the analysis of dreams, and I have studied them. Listening to angels was not a dream for me. I remember.

Sunshine and warmth filled the day. It was an afternoon. I was waiting for my friend, Stephen, to come out and play. I was wearing a red and white striped jersey. My mother must have liked that jersey because I see it in many of that time's photographs. Or maybe I didn't have that many shirts. It sounds crazy, but I still believe I heard those angelic choirs singing. Perhaps, it was just Mrs. Shaw playing an old record on her player, and she had it tuned up really loud. Maybe it was St. Peter himself, sharing alleluia with me. I don't know. I do know I remember the experience. It remains authentic to me today as if it was just yesterday. Perhaps, the closeness of death and the unpredictable reality of sudden sickness and mortality keep me wondering what life is all about.

I am like the old hermit, bent with the weight of so many years, walking silently along his wooded path. The shaded wood keeps his thoughts cool, but just like Alfie, from another time, he keeps wondering. I have a keen sense of sadness about myself. I also have a consciousness of glad peace. I sometimes stop near a neighborhood school and watch the children play in a wooded area near where I walk. They run along the paths, not sure where exactly to go but not afraid of their direction. I know there are Black bears in these woods. One chased me once. I ran to the top of a baseball bleacher, thinking this might somehow be protection. These young ones are not so foolish or concerned, and they are not afraid. I was like that once, running with my twin brother down the gray cement sidewalks of a large city street. I remember flying down the long steep hill on an old pair of roller skates, totally unconcerned about the possibility of a fall, even though I would have a few of them too. Life was not so fragile then. I smile at those memories. They seem almost imaginary as I recall them now. I had another experience that was also very unbelievable. It was not a possible dream, though. It was a nightmare, and I would almost die. This scene would come to haunt me. My recollection of a recent horrible death on a winding wet road would soon crash into my memory. I saw a large truck come careening into my cruiser, crashing head-on into my life. There was smoke, and I could not move. It was not a dream.

Chapter Sixteen: Rain, Rain Go Away

It looked like rain might come that day. I remember driving into work for A Squad, and the sky was becoming very cloudy. "Rain, rain, go away, come again another day." My reflections and memories remind me sometimes of raindrops. Crystal tears often blanket my recollections. I have loved writing since I was a young man in seminary high school, and I have described them in several different ways throughout my years. They are unique, precious drops of my life in other times and the experiences of those days. Some of those that I have reflected on are seen in my poetry. Others I write about today. I think I began way back in the high school seminary. I had an English teacher named Fr. Hart, who often told me to "Keep writing. You have a gift." He eventually had me write articles and submissions to local newspapers. I somehow remember he submitted some of my writing to a student contest in the *Hartford Times*. I think I may have won an Honorable Mention once upon a time. My awareness reminds me that in many of my poems, even those written in the massive study hall of a seminary high school, the reality of raindrops always hinted at sorrow and weeping. They surely did on this day.

My life changed on one such sunless day filled with many sad raindrops. I had looked forward to perhaps another four or five years in the police department. Some months before, I had hit 20 years of service and still loved my work. My career was not a planned reality of set goals and aspirations. The thought of retirement had not entered my mind, and I had no plans to do that. My primary career benchmark was making money and catching up with others in my age group. When I left the priesthood, I returned from Argentina with eleven U.S. dollars in my pocket. I was in my early thirties then, and by that time, most men and women had been earning regular paychecks for ten years. They had savings as well. I had neither until I became a cop. My goal was also to live a comfortable life with my wife and family. I would eventually do that. In those days, I was trying to catch up with my age group in the amount of savings and security that I might have. This goal meant I spent many days working 12-hour shifts when I could. I also took an occasional extra job, like directing traffic at a construction site or making sure pedestrians got across the streets near their various houses of worship. These days also included 12-hour shifts, with 8-hour breaks between work schedules.

Most cops I knew worked their asses off for the last three years of their careers. Overtime incomes consistently increased retirement figures. That had been my plan, although not for a few years. I looked forward to that time in my career when I could add significant overtime to my salary and look forward to a less stressed daily schedule in the recesses of my mind. I looked forward to a future time when my life might be more comfortable and my days less hectic. Reality would change that day. Comfort would not be a part of any future for many months.

I love driving motorcycles, but I don't love getting soaked. The day was turning colder and clouding into darker gray clouds. There was a hint of rain in the air. I remember regret as I turned around on the motorcycle and headed back to the station to grab a cruiser to finish my shift. I went back to the station and switched vehicles. I did not know it then, but that decision changed much more than the vehicles I drove that day. I warmed up my car and headed for a coffee at McDonald's. I know the stereotype of cops and donuts, but I love coffee, not donuts. I drove from the headquarters and listened to the radio as I called the dispatcher that I was clear from the station and heading for District 3, my assignment for the day. I turned onto the roadway and headed home for lunch instead of my local coffee shop. I hadn't been there for a while. I didn't trust a young lady who worked there. I had recently arrested her and two of her friends for shoplifting at a local mall, and I did not trust that coffee would be the only ingredient entering my cup of java. I decided that not going to coffee was not such a big deal after all.

I loved my house and going home whenever possible while on duty. It was a light brown log cabin that my wife and I had purchased a few years before. Colorful wildflowers grew among the boulders which lined the front yard. I had planted many of these myself and especially loved seeing them as they grew between the rocks and boulders of the welcoming hill. Our home had a large front porch extending the whole house's width. I loved seeing the view of the seven white rocking chairs that spread across this front porch. Memories of family and friends enjoying this spot always made me smile as I drove up our long driveway. I loved entertaining here, and it was not unusual to find visitors' cars parked there as I maneuvered to my garage. It was also not uncommon to see a delivery truck. My wife is very outgoing, with a beautiful personality, just perfect for sales. She was a top seller for Tupperware. She had won many awards and had her own successful sales team who worked under her banner. The white van in our driveway symbolized her success, as the company had given it to her for outstanding sales. The brown delivery truck coming out of our driveway was a familiar vehicle, also a symbol of her achievements, as it delivered more household goods and products to be offered or sold at the next sales meeting.

I smiled as I saw this truck about to exit my drive. I was sure that more clear plastic bowls and other containers with their blue and red lids had just been delivered. I stopped and waited for the oncoming traffic to pass and for the delivery vehicle to drive from my log house entrance. I remember that the road had begun to ice up a bit. I remember the green flashing of the left turn signal light on my dashboard, which I had turned on as I approached my home. I saw the car in the oncoming lane stop to let the delivery truck into the roadway. It was a silver car, and I remember thinking, what a nice guy to be so polite. The world needed more people like this. Then I also saw the large white box truck in the oncoming lane. It was about five football fields away. It was traveling fast, much too fast for the wet icing condition of the road. The back of the truck began to slide, and I knew the driver was losing control. I remember thinking, "That asshole is going to hit that Toyota, and I am going to miss lunch." I imagined the accident that was about to happen right before me. "What a shithead." I hated car accidents. I disliked writing the accident reports they always involved, especially drawing the diagrams that showed what happened. I hated them, especially when they happened when I was about to have lunch. I did not realize at that moment that I would become the accident I dreaded.

Chapter Seventeen: Gray Day

I think of that day now. It was dreary and gray. I look back to that moment with the distance of so many years, and it all seems like I am watching a slow-motion video from some crazy YouTube channel I have never joined. I see the woods shrouded in a light mist on the right side of the road. The Farmington River flows beyond them. It is not too far from the road, and I can hear the waters going by. It is not too deep in this area, and I had seen fly fishers there on a previous day, angling for some speckled trout. On the other side of the street, across from the river view, solitary mailboxes stood along the roadway. They indicated the hidden driveways of homes situated further into the woods. It all seems like a blur to me. I saw the river on the right, the mailboxes on the left, and the large white truck suddenly sliding into my lane. The face of the driver was hidden behind the black-colored wipers, slowly moving back and forth on the front window, painting his panic in the blur of the wet windshield. His mouth was wide open, and I almost heard his scream. I see his hands on the steering wheel, tightly wrapped fingers trying to control the uncontrollable 30,000-pound box truck. Then I see the front of that truck crossing into my lane and careening towards my cruiser. I can see its back sliding back and forth as the vehicle careened towards my cruiser. I remember saying, "Oh, fuck," just before it crashed head-on into my cruiser.

I did not believe what I was seeing. This out-of-control truck was crashing into my car! I remember the feeling of impact as the front end of my cruiser crumbled, and suddenly the airbag smashed into my body. The steering wheel pressed against my chest, and I could not move. The airbag had locked me into the seat. I felt pain in my back and legs. A tremendous panic struck when I realized I could not move. My feet were locked and trapped under the brake and gas pedals. I was not able to move. I would feel a lot of pain later.

The firewall of my cruiser crashed into my legs. The airbag exploded into my chest, and suddenly I was pinned against the seat, with the steering wheel locked against my chest. I had to twist my body somehow to grab the mic to call for help. The collision contorted my arm somehow behind my back. I began to smell burning oil and saw smoke seeping into the car's passenger area. It was coming from under the glove compartment. I had recently gone to a pickup truck fire and had a sudden, horrible flashback to that incident. A man had died in those flames as he screamed and burned to death before me. I remember trying again to reach for the radio, bending to my right, and finally grabbing the microphone.

I was so relieved that I could push the button. I was finally able to contact the station. I advised the dispatcher that I had been in an accident, that I was hurt, and that my vehicle was on fire. One sergeant who was on duty that day remembers that call vividly. She recently told me her first response was disbelief when she heard that transmission over the air. This officer listened to my voice, and I sounded faint and afraid. She told me that she could listen to my fear and was stunned. She had never known me to be scared, ever. The dispatcher responded that help was on the way, and I listened to my speakers explode with radio calls to various firehouses and police districts. Fire trucks, ambulances, and my brothers and sisters were on their way. I felt a tremendous sense of relief. I knew what was going on at that moment. Lights and sirens were being activated all over the town and speeding along the many streets that separated us. The cavalry was on the way at high speed. Throughout my career, I was part of that team, responding to serious motor vehicle crashes. I was that call today, helpless, in pain, and very frightened. I was also grateful to hear those sirens in the distance.

My wife had heard the crash. She thought it might be the UPS delivery truck just leaving our driveway. When Donna called the station to report that she heard what sounded like a possible car crash, the dispatcher thought she already knew it was me. She did not. The kind dispatcher reassured her, "Don't worry, Donna, everyone is on the way. Chick will be o.k." She ran out of the house, and I saw her running down our long driveway. The truck driver who had just smashed into me was also running toward my location. They both got to my car around the same time and tried unsuccessfully to open the door. I was terrified that the car would soon ignite in flames, and I did not want her near it. I screamed at her to stop coming near my car, and the approaching sirens drowned out my wife's shouts. I felt a tremendous sense of relief that help had arrived. I did not know my injuries then. I did know, though, that I would soon be out of that car.

A web of darkness and light holds my memories tightly. Panic and fear sometimes invite obscurity. I have also found that remembered thoughts of hope and relief occasionally call for a clear view of those past times. I can step into parts of that day as if they happened just yesterday. Other moments of that day remain in the blackness of my hurts and pain. I am hardly conscious of them at all. I remember my wife's cries. I heard her calling my name in a much more panicked sound than the sirens. I also heard wailing in the distance. Yet I do not recall the many police officers and first responders who rushed to this scene. They surrounded my wife with care and concern and got her away from the car. The police chief responded to the scene and ensured a female officer was with my wife for the rest of that day. This was the same person who had introduced Donna to me. God works in strange ways sometimes.

I do not remember any of that. I do remember the harried firefighters working to open my crashed cruiser. I remember the tremendous relief I felt when they lifted the mangled hood and doused the engine compartment with retardant. I would find out later that the smoke that filled my cruiser was from motor oil dripping all over the hot cruiser engine. It was not on fire and probably would not have ignited. I did not know that then, but seeing those guys fill that engine area with some white foam was a tremendous relief. I remember when they finally got my door open.

The impact of the collision had caused my driver's side door to buckle. I think they used a crowbar and the strength of four firefighters to finally pull the door open. I remember voices. One of them asked if I was alive. My eyes were closed, so I got the question. I do not remember seeing any faces.

I was a crazy contortion. The brake and gas pedals had pinned my legs against the firewall. The impact had contorted my body to the right, and I could feel my weapon pushing against my hip. My right arm had somehow become locked behind my back, and I remember breathing was very painful. I would later find that a significant amount of muscle and ligament damage was the reason for this, but I had no fractures. I heard someone off in the distance radio headquarters telling them to have Life Star respond as soon as possible. Cops have sardonic humor. We all knew that a call for this rescue helicopter was the best hope for an injured victim whose condition was not hopeful. Many of us referred to that rescue chopper as Death Star, and I knew very well at that moment what my condition appeared to be. I heard the dispatcher respond that the helicopter had been grounded and would not be responding because of the rainy weather of the day. The poor visibility of the moment made landing near my scene too dangerous. Many months later, I spoke with one of the Life Star nurses. The whole crew felt absolute frustration at their inability to fly that day. I remember kidding with her as I asked, "Imagine how I felt when I heard you weren't on your way?" A year later, that young nurse would be killed when that helicopter crashed while responding to another accident.

I was in and out of consciousness in the ambulance. I could hear the siren as we headed for the trauma unit at Hartford Hospital. It was nine miles away, but we would be there very soon. I remember a female paramedic refusing to let go of my hand. I had known her for many years, and we had shared emergencies. She kept reassuring me that I was going to be okay. The next thing I remember was I was on a table in the emergency room. There was a nurse there who was cutting off my clothes. I knew her from

Unionville, and I remember feeling self-conscious as she cut off the last vestiges of my clothing, including my underwear. They must have given me some pain medications because the only memories I have of those hours in the emergency room were sometimes hearing the voices of First Responders and cops way beyond the curtain. They sounded very far in the distance. My daughter, Marci, pulled that curtain back. I smile now at this memory. I don't think a concrete wall would have kept her from seeing me. I must have been nodding off. My eyes were closed, and she gingerly touched my foot to let me know of her presence. I screamed in pain. We laugh about this now. At the time, it was not funny at all.

Chapter Eighteen: Tough Times

Physical therapy and other medical professional visits filled many days after I went home from the hospital. This routine went on for months, but from my view, it seemed like way more than that. At the start of my rehabilitation, I had PT three times a week. I remember how painful it was, just sitting in the car while Donna drove me. She tried to be as careful as possible, but every bump, for many weeks, resulted in pain for me. Eventually, the discomfort of those rides gave way to relaxed anticipation, as those rides became much easier, as well as the PT exercises. Then there were the appointments for the various pain management doctors. I did not want to take highly addictive pain medications, and my orthopedic surgeon suggested acupuncture and self-hypnosis. They worked for me. The frustration of my slow-moving and unbending legs eventually gave way to the great satisfaction of walking near the Farmington River with my good friend Vincent Trantolo. He kidded me that I was getting faster than him. I so appreciated his kindness. The blackness of heavy depression had filled my days since my accident. Light would eventually replace that, as an insightful psychiatrist helped me see that there could be smiles, even in tears. Finally, after all of those months, walking became more manageable. I even began to run slowly, improving physically and emotionally. I started to believe in a healing tomorrow. I finally accepted that my pain might be a summons to a better time. I took that invitation.

I had become an expert architect during those times. I was an exquisite builder of walls and successfully used unique materials. The darkened matter of my soul created the bricks, blocks, and mortar of these structures. My painful hurts and waves of anger and fears were the high walls that had come to separate me from my wife and many others who cared for me. I finally began to destroy these structures and began to be a bridge-builder. Eventually, I started reaching out to my wife, daughter, and many relatives and friends who had stood by me during my healing. My gratitude for them began to replace all of the bitterness of the past many months. I wanted them to know how thankful I was for their patience with me, a sometime very unpleasant patient. I had finally reached what euphemistically was called my MMI, also known as my maximum medical improvement. I wasn't going to be getting any better, but I certainly had come a long way from those days of being much worse.

I looked forward to my last visit with my orthopedic doctor. He was a surgeon and had become a very close friend during this whole time. He was the all-star quarterback who had directed all of the various plays of my multiple treatments and rehabs. He had brought me to the finish line, and I anxiously waited to hear from him for his winning call. That would not be. I remember sitting in his office with Donna. I had butterflies in my stomach while waiting to speak with the doctor. I was looking forward to his words permitting me to get back to cop duty.

The doctor could not approve my return to work. He reviewed my injuries. He read about the lack of full arm extension, some disc compression near the top of my spine, and possible damages resulting from harmful future confrontations. I could no longer be a police officer. My memory of that moment is crisp and almost always new to me. I stood up from my chair in shock, and my wife did too. She held me. I had been laughing with Donna just a few minutes before this conversation. My smiles were replaced by tears that reflected weeping in that room. The doctor cried too. There were no touchdowns that day.

Many destinations would eventually stretch out before me. When I left the priesthood, the only direction I moved toward was the one that brought me to the world of law enforcement. After my cop career, I had to find another path. I would no longer be involved with the roll calls I had attended for twenty years. Arresting drunk drivers disappeared from my daily routine. I would not break up any more bar fights. There would be no more criminal investigations for me. The close fellowship that daily danger causes to grow with cops would end. I no longer experienced the real pride and joy I had known as I protected and served the people of my community.

This memoir is not some resume. As you can see, I have had the opportunity for many experiences. These words have been about my road trip through my days, not yet done. I am not a secret keeper but a traveler. You are an explorer, too, with your twists and turns along the way. I seek to teach about my journey, feelings and thoughts, insights, and maybe even some small amount of wisdom. Ultimately, I have found my way.

Eventually, I became a substitute teacher. I would once again experience the absolute joy I had known as a teacher, those so many years ago, as a young priest. I knew many of the high school kids sitting in my various classes. I should say most of them at least knew of me. Most of them were good kids, filled with their hopes and dreams as they tried to figure out their wanderings into their futures. I had a good reputation with them and our times together were a lot of fun for me. I think they may have learned something too. I hope so. I have always loved the study of psychology and have had considerable experience in counseling. I eventually became a part of a psychologist's family practice, where I once again put on my helper hat, doing individual and family therapy. I know I assisted many during this time. More to the point, though, many people helped me. I realized every day that I was way more than a job description. I was a part of significant transactions where honest communication and transparency were critical to communication and growth.

I eventually even got elected to two terms on the Farmington Town Council. I have a great sense of humor. When I tell people about this achievement, I share that this voting says more about the mental health of Farmington's citizens than my abilities. I am convinced that my first election resulted from sympathy for me as an injured former police officer. When I got re-elected, I understood that many citizens thought I had done good things for this beautiful town. I hope so.

There was also that time when my wife and I became the owners of a package store, a location where people could purchase alcohol. It was called a "package" store because some legislator had decided many years ago that purchases must be hidden in bags. I realized very quickly that this retail environment was not for me. My wife loved it. I had little tolerance for people more interested in buying lottery tickets than bottles of Cabernet. Thank God Donna had patience. Thank God I also got to work in a prestigious personal injury law firm. This environment allowed me to escape from that little package store to the larger milieu of personal injury law. I was involved with investigations initially, and then public relations and marketing. Eventually, I would be an advisor to attorneys, staff, and clients, about being their best and doing their best, even during the most challenging times. I had been an accident victim and could share my perceptions of that experience with them. I had experienced negative times, but I could still say, "Yes, I can" to all of my tomorrows. Again, I was teaching, I was preaching, I was protecting, but most of all, I was serving.

I know that my attitude determines it all. I choose to be positive or negative, loving and forgiving, or judgmental and critical. Experience tells me that seldom are these choices easy—my faith and personal philosophy demand that I try at least to be my very best. Hopefully, my actions have echoed that. If I choose to settle for being less than I know I can be, that is a decision for negativity. There are enough negative people in this world, and I choose not to walk with them. They are poisonous. I have decided there are certain things that I have to do to keep on keeping on. I keep my life simple. After many years, I finally realized that drama belongs in theaters, not in my life. I decide every day to stay positive. I don't know how many tomorrows I have, and all of my yesterdays are gone. Today is my day. I have learned that I need to define specific goals for myself and act on them.

Otherwise, I float through my day. I know that talk is cheap. Accomplishment takes work. One of the most important lessons along my way is to stay away from toxic people. They are poison. Some have caused me to lose my way at times. They are joy stealers and darkness for my soul. I am a student, always. I have learned that others have a great deal to teach me. I believe, humbly with Einstein, that we can either think that nothing is a miracle or everything is. I choose that everything is, as long as we have the eyes to look and finally to see.

This much I know. Authentic life demands genuine care. I cannot care for someone else unless I learn to take care of myself first. I know that caring for you means caring for me first. Psychology and theology have taught me that I cannot say yes to another until I first say yes to myself.

The goal of love is to accept another without condition

Self-acceptance makes this a possibility. I know that caring means that I am open to the possible. My promise convinces my future of meaning. Stilting doubt has no place in my walk towards tomorrow. "Yes, I can" is always my proclamation. I know that care also means being brave.

I need to be tenacious in all that I attempt. I know my God calls me to be my best and to do my best. Sometimes, this takes guts. I do not give up on my journey to become more than I am at this very moment. I know that care demands that I have a sense of humor. I need to be able to laugh at myself and with others. Laughter is critical for me to enjoy my life. It also helps others to smile as well. I know that care explains me. Nothing I do is without meaning. All of my actions, or lack of them, have implications. How I care for myself and others is my ultimate definition. I know that care empowers me to act. There is no such thing as inertia in life. I know that care is a commitment. Psychology has a well-known triangle of dysfunction; Blaming (finding fault), Bullying (causing hurt), and Buying (manipulating). I want to be without all of these. I know, though, that they have been a part of the sometimes-tattered clothes I have worn along my cobbled way. They have affected my relationship with myself, others, and God. This much I know.

My physical, mental, and spiritual health are critical to my success as a human being. I either say yes to all I am and choose to be or decide to say no to all of my potential and growth. I know that this care requires acknowledgment. It means genuine care for someone else. We must lift one another and tear down the dark, ugly walls of judgment and criticism. I know that care means concern. There is no place for long pauses in finding out what my hopes and dreams are. I prefer small steps in the sunshine of promise to standing still in the darkness of doubt and fear. And so, I continue to walk.

Chapter Nineteen: Alive

Riding a mountain bike saved my life. I am Farmington's first Community Police Officer. I am also the first certified bike cop. I had gone through grueling and extensive training with other selected officers from agencies throughout the state. Our instructors were certified by the International Mountain Bike Police Association, and they demanded excellence and peak performance from each student. Many of our days were filled with hours of riding up steep paved roads and learning to navigate narrow dirt paths, speeding down a rock-filled mountainside. I was very proud when I successfully completed this training. Some officers did not. When I got back on duty, there were many days when I would pedal thirty or forty miles around the Unionville section of town.

Little did I realize as I rode those many streets that this exertion probably saved my life. The attending physician in the Hartford Hospital emergency room thought so. I also had torn ligaments, some nerve damage, and many muscle tears. I had severe strains in my hands and my feet. There were significant back and shoulder injuries as well, as my body registered some of the damage resulting from the impact of a 26,000-pound box truck. I could wiggle my toes and touch my nose. I realized I had more years ahead of me to rock the boat. I did not know, though, at that time, that the vessel of my proud police career was sinking and that it would come to an end. This crash had wrecked more than my cruiser and more than some of my muscles, nerves, and ligaments. The doctors were concerned about a severe concussion and compression injuries to the upper part of my spine. The emergency room doctor told me that I was a fortunate guy. If my police car had been moving, even at a slow roll, when the crash happened, paralysis might have been the result.

I was not dying. I heard some of the paramedics and first responders at the scene. They were whispering among themselves. They thought I would not make it. They did not know then, but I had no internal bleeding. My significantly damaged cruiser informed their view. The head-on crash had destroyed my car, and it looked like I must have had some severe injuries. I did, but I had no significant life-threatening injuries at the time. Those who had responded to the scene could not see that at the time. I had no fractures. There was no internal bleeding. I remember my eyes clenched and just feeling pain all over.

I was rolled out of the emergency room to the neurological intensive care unit for observation and treatment. I remember looking across from my room, where some nurses were attending to another patient. A white sheet covered most of his body. Bandages that seeped blood were wrapped around his head. He looked like a mummy. He was still, and I never saw him move. Looking at him, I knew I was in much better shape than he was. He did not look like he would leave the hospital. I knew that I was eventually going home. I also remember being petrified about whatever my condition might be. I must have had some more pain meds because I soon fell asleep. When I woke up, I looked at where this other patient had been. He was no longer there. A nurse told me that he had been a gunshot victim.

A bullet had ripped into his head, and he had died. Life is so fragile. There but for fortune is such a good insight for each of us. I never knew the facts about this shooting. That person could have been an innocent bystander to a violent crime, or perhaps a gang member caught up in the street violence all around us. It didn't matter anymore. There would be no more dreams for him. I knew that no matter what my tomorrow might bring, there would be dreams of better times on some future night. The nurse also told me to get some rest. Tomorrow, a significant neurological evaluation awaited me. I was going to have a considerable exam. I might have to say the alphabet backward. She laughed and explained that she could not release me because of my severe concussion until I had passed a memory test. I had visions of staying there forever.

The next day, Abe Lincoln saved me. A very comical Intern pulled back the curtains of my area and gave me a bunch of remembering tests. He enjoyed telling me that I would remain his patient until I passed. I did not find his humor funny and was very concerned about my ability to recollect. I remember having to count backward from one hundred and subtracting a certain number after each count. I told the Intern that on my best days, this would be tough for me. He then asked me to name Presidents in order from the present backward. I got back to Theodore Roosevelt, and the doc was quite impressed. So was I. One of the last questions he asked was, "Who was the president that freed the slaves?" I got that question right, too, and the Intern told me I was about to be released from the hospital. I was still in a significant amount of pain. Several months of physical therapy and some surgeries to repair ligament damage were ahead of me. I knew, though, that I had many more mornings in front of me, unlike that young man who had shared a neurological intensive care unit with me. I was going to be leaving this hospital very soon. The orderly got me into a wheelchair in a few hours and wheeled me out the front door. Donna would help me into our car. I would be in pain still, but hopeful that I could meet whatever challenges faced me in my unknown tomorrow. At least I knew that I had such a future. That young man who had been with me had none.

My mind has always been a crazy multicolored kaleidoscope of imagination and memory. I often place myself in other people's lives and wonder about living in their space. I am curious about what it might be like to walk in someone else's shoes. I do not do this to escape the guy I call myself. I laugh at the thought that some psychologists might disagree with me. I do this more to understand the people I have met along my road. As I left Hartford Hospital, I pictured that young person who had died in the intensive care unit. I guessed what his life might have been as my wife drove us back to the comfort and safety of our suburban home. I never lived in a house where giant ugly rats competed for space in the kitchen with little brothers or sisters. I never went to sleep smelling the residue of an overflowed toilet not working because a landlord or some overworked or lazy building inspector had not scheduled time for a repair to an ancient, finally cracked pipe. It still stunk even after all a working mother's efforts to clean. I never lived with the stereotype of being lazy because I was poor. I never had the experience of being stopped while walking or driving in a "white" neighborhood because I "matched the description" of someone who had committed a crime.

I have imagined what it must have been like for my boyhood friend who joined the Marines as an 18-year-old kid trying to get away from an asshole father. I think of him cold in the rain of a monsoon season in Vietnam, shivering in fear as darkness surrounded him and his platoon and Viet Cong trying to kill him. I can smell the vomit near his foxhole. There is dried blood all around and the rotting flesh of dead soldiers. I feel the tears streaming down his dirty, unshaven face as body bags filled with his friends pile up. Somehow, I know his sense of guilt all these years later, as he speaks of having made it "off that hill" with so few of his brothers.

I have even imagined Anne Frank as she hid for two years from the Nazis with eight other family members and friends in an 850-square-foot factory hiding place. They hoped to evade capture by the Nazis who had invaded and prowled their city of Amsterdam in the horror of World War II. I wonder what it was like for her to look out a two-inch slice of the window, see blue sky and red birds nearby, and hope one day to walk outside again. I wonder about her feelings as she lay dying of Typhus, on a filthy, lice-ridden bunk, in the nightmare place called Bergen-Belsen. Her father, Otto Frank, had once given her the gift of a diary, and she named her journal "Kitty." As she lived all the horror of a death camp, I wonder if she remembered the words she had written so many months before. "I don't think of all the misery but all the beauty that remains." I hope so. Somehow, those words always hint to me of God's presence in my life and world. They make possible my ability to speak "Yes, I can," even when I can only whisper those words. I know there is a God as long as there is a hint of goodness in my experience. There always has been.

I firmly believe that my life has been about figuring out God's will for me. Ultimately, I think this search for my meaning and yours comes down to knowing somehow in our gut whether the place we are is the best place for us. It is about knowing on a deep level that there is a sense of peace about who I finally am and who I am becoming. I understand that each one of us is unique. I realize some of us are actually in situations where realities like illness and poverty seem so much to shrink our possibilities. To a degree, I know what that means. I have to a limited degree, lived such experiences. Even now, I know that God calls us to become more aware of who we are and who He calls us to become, to grow into our best selves.

In the many days of my rehabilitation after I left the hospital, I discovered that my injuries caused me to learn new lessons, like how to depend on someone. There were times when I was furious at my reality, my wounds, my wife, and the doctors, and I had to learn patience. During those times when I wanted to give up, I knew in a brand-new way that each day was a challenge to say "yes" or "no." I chose to affirm my life, even in the uncertainty of my tomorrow. I believe that each of us is a gift to one another. We each have skills that life calls us to share. I know that somehow existence beckons me and each of us to be more than we are. My faith is relational. I experience my God in my relationships with the people He places in my life. I think this is what faith is all about for me. He calls me to constantly bloom in the garden of my life as I try to become more loving, forgiving, faith-filled, and hopeful. I left the priesthood because I finally understood that God certainly did not want me to live so unhappily and confused. None of us has been given such a calling, and not one of us should choose such an experience. We all have so many doors to open into new pathways. My sad realization is that sometimes I have been afraid to turn the knob while standing alone in the darkness. Some portals are complicated to walk, though. My exit from the priesthood was like that. Sometimes, life makes difficult choices for us. That is what I found as I had to walk out of the blue door of law enforcement. Even in those hesitant steps, I whispered, "Yes, I can."

Chapter Twenty: Keep On Keeping On

Many important insights have become part of my life in the many years I have walked my way. Forgiveness is a central tenet for me. I was blessed with the experience of reconciliation with my parents. I do not think they ever understood why I left the priesthood, but I do know they spent the rest of their lives very proud of me and the choices I had made. They felt the same way about my brother, Bill. I was with each one of them when they passed away. They knew very well my love for them and I knew their love for me. Family is about love and forgiveness. I have learned that sometimes those realities take time. They also demand a relationship based on acceptance and a refusal to judge.

Faith is central to my life, and a person named Jesus is central to my belief. I have no certainty about Him or His divinity. I have doubts and sometimes don't even know how to pray. In the silence of unanswered prayers, I still live in hope. I look at the cosmos and the myriads of nature's wonders and believe there is a loving creator, a reality beyond my understanding. I think love is eternal, and I am aware my personal experience of affirmation is incomplete and imperfect.

I look forward to a time when that experience of affirmation and acceptance is total.

This is my hope, and I will continue my journey. Sit with me on my favorite park bench. Remember, it's an old green seat with fading, blistered paint. Be careful, though. I must warn you about slivers. My reflecting place is still near that sparkling pond I loved to be near, even after all of these years. Walk over the ancient, cobbled bridge and join me. The chair remains where it has always been, unmoved.

I look forward to meeting you there.

I invite you to treasure this day. Do not just look at flowers. Touch them and breathe them and appreciate their unique beauty. I have learned to slow down and enjoy all of God's blessings. That includes the people He has placed in my life. As you might have guessed by now, I am far from perfect. There have been times in my life when I have been very selfish, sometimes at the expense of others. I have broken promises to myself and others. I also have kept them. I believe in a loving and forgiving God, and I can finally love and forgive myself. I am dedicated to staying upbeat. I have discovered that kindness is always the better choice, even when such a choice is tough.

There is so much negativity in our world. I have met negative people, and I am grateful to them. This sounds crazy, but they have taught me magnificent lessons. The most forgiving people are not those who wore the expensive coat of judgment but those who suffered the lonely sadness of being judged. I am not a stranger to rude people or those who are hurtful. Many have introduced themselves to me, sometimes hidden in the guise of kindness. I do not want their dysfunction. I have lived too much sadness and shed too many tears.

I try to keep negativity out of my life. I avoid self-centered people who tend to brag and gossip. They have two conversations: building themselves up or tearing someone else down. Some are acquaintances, and a few are even family members. You can recognize these people. They seldom smile, and when they laugh, it is usually at someone else. I try hard to keep away from their darkness. Drama belongs in the theatre. I do not want it in my life. I suggest you keep it out of your journey as well. I believe in the possible. There have been times when I was lost and confused. I know because I have trod, like a vagabond, alone and afraid. These pages have shared some of those times.

There is an old bar where a fat lady waits her turn at the mike. It is hard to tell her age. She is almost ageless. I can see a small stage, off in the distance, in the middle of a not-so-small area. Many people are walking near the platform. Some young people are running around and having a good time, and some teenagers are off in a corner laughing at a private joke. Most of the crowd is older, though. There is a window way up on the back wall. It's not very clean and seems like it hasn't been washed in ages. Dust covers some panes, and there are cobwebs in the corners. There is a beautiful view of the ocean beyond. Off in the quiet corner, there are people sharing secrets and soft talk. The tables are small, and the place is crowded. The waiters and waitresses are busy, and the smell of comfort food fills the air. Some people are dancing to the tunes of the various entertainers. Sad songs invite close dancing with touching bodies and hearts, and distant memories live in those embraces, too. It's a lively place. It reminds me of the Cheers bar in Boston, where "everybody knows your name."

I keep looking for that heavy-set woman, and I finally see her. She's outside smoking a cigarette with one or two others. The smoke clouds around them. It smells pungent. It's starting to get dark out there, and I see a light rainfall. She is coming in and has a glass in her right hand. It's bigger than a shot glass, but not a mug. I think it might be whiskey. She sips it and nods, smiling to some and waving to others entering the door. She seems to be having a good time over there by the entrance. I think she must be a "regular" because everyone stops to say hello. She has the door partly open and keeps inviting others in. Patrons have introduced themselves and are sharing drinks and smiles. Two couples wearing leather jackets decorated with skulls and crossbones are laughing and lining up for the stage. A guy with dreadlocks and a red polo shirt is joining them. I can't wait for them to sing, but first, I am going outside to see their bikes.

I see the Master of Ceremonies, and he is almost six feet, but it's hard to figure out how old he is. Someone sitting near the front row said his name is Peter. He is dressed in an immaculate white suit, a beautiful sky-blue shirt, with a bright, joyful, multicolored tie. He's bathed in some soft golden light, coming from above, maybe from way high over the stage. I am not sure. The shadows are playing with my mind, though. I even imagine there is a crucifix on the wall. This guy is smiling and very approachable. He is sociable, and lots of people talk with him. I walk through the crowd, wave my hand to him and ask when the show concludes. He looks at me with a knowing smile and yells through all the laughter, the smiles, and the joy, "Hey Chick, it is not over until the fat lady sings." I cannot believe it. He knew my name.

I still wait for the fat lady to sing. I have more to do. There are more challenges to face, more people to meet, and more experiences and memories to savor.

"Yes, I can."

About the Author

Chick Pritchard began his studies for the Catholic priesthood when he entered the seminary as a fourteen- year old boy. Twelve years later, he was ordained a Catholic priest.   His years in the clergy were filled with the immense satisfaction which comes from helping others. There was also a lingering doubt and deep sense of sadness that lived in his heart as well. After much soul-searching, Chick left the ministry and became a cop. He was a highly respected police officer, selected for many honors, including several Proclamations from the State of CT recognizing his outstanding career in law enforcement.   His time on duty ended in a cruiser crash, which also began many new chapters in Chick's life. He was twice elected to the Farmington, CT Town Council. He has been a successful teacher, business consultant, and public speaker who has mentored hundreds of people from all walks of life. This is the inspiring and deeply personal story of his life, its doubts, fears, hopes, and joys. This memoir is about the success of a man very honest with himself and with his God.

Chick lives in Weatogue, CT with his wife Donna. They have eight wonderful grandchildren, Logan, Jakob, Alex, Aly, Jessica, Cayden, Ella, and Tyler, who are all unique and loved very much. Chick continues to keep on keeping on.

MAYBE......

Candy apple red and yellow balloons....And ice cream and sugar cones......and blue flowers that whisper good morning but never goodbye....maybe that's what life is all about...and Noah's ark is on its way....God's breath but a whisper upon this dust we call man.....meaning...lack of meaning....what's it all about......Candy apple red and yellow balloons and ice cream and sugar cones.....and blue flowers that whisper good morning.....but never goodbye..... Maybe that's what life is all about......CP

Thank you for reading my book. I would be grateful if you might visit the site where you purchased my memoir and write a brief review. Your rating and comment are important to me and will help others decide to read my book as well.

Made in the USA
Middletown, DE
12 May 2023